SEP - - 2019

NO LONGER PROPERTY OF
SEATTLE PUBLIC LIBRARY

D0548728

NINJA

GET GOOD

MY ULTIMATE GUIDE TO GAMING

TYLER BLEVINS

with WILL PARTIN

Clarkson Potter/Publishers
New York

FOR JESSICA

CONTENTS

READER,

A few things before we drop in. The book you're holding was designed with a single idea in mind: what I wish I had known about gaming when I was starting to get serious about it.

This isn't really meant to be the kind of book you pick up and read starting on the first page and ending on the last, though you can do that if you want. It's more like a reference book—an encyclopedia, by me, for gamers like us. It's a compendium of some of the tips and tricks I've collected over the years, arranged in one place so that you can look to it when you need some guidance on the little things or the big ones. Whether you're brand-new to gaming, or you're a grizzled veteran, I think you'll learn something new.

The best place for a book like this is right by your computer or your console. It's meant to be used, not just read and then put on the shelf. You can look at it when you have questions or feel stuck. Revisit it occasionally to see if you learn something new. Write your own tips or discoveries in the margins, and dog-ear pages you find especially useful. If you ever ask me to sign your copy, I want to see that you've really put it to use.

There are a couple content features in here you should know about before you start reading. "Hot Fix!" boxes explain quick ways to address common errors, while boxes marked "Ninja's Way" are specific illustrations of how I personally handle the challenges that I'll describe in more abstract terms in the main text. There are also exercises and even a little game. Finally, I've added a list of resources at the back that you can check out once you think you've exhausted what I've written here. There's only so much you can say in a single book, so I want you to know where you can go when you're ready to take your game to the next level.

Unlike games, you only get one chance when it comes to books, so I've tried to make the wisdom in here as timeless as possible. That means I don't talk much about how to play *specific* games. Instead, I talk about gaming. I'll use *Fortnite*, *Apex Legends*, and plenty of other games as examples throughout the book, but most of the content in here is meant to be bigger than any one game. Games come and go, and you'll have to go with them. But if you pay attention to the lessons in this book, you'll find that you're never really starting over. Who knows—maybe you'll even beat me someday. Or not. That's up to you.

See You In-Game,

Ninja

Tyler

GEAR UP. ①

Every gamer relies on hardware. Like power plants or electricity, it's the foundation that makes gaming possible, and when our equipment is working, we don't have to think about it at all. **Mice, keyboards, and headsets should feel like a natural part of your body, so that you can trust your tools.** Believe me: there's nothing worse than knowing you lost a game because your equipment failed you. Losses like that are demotivating and, more important, when you're trying to get better, they're opportunities lost.

Monitor, page 25

Headset, page 28

Mouse, page 18

Mechanical Keyboard, page 14

But even if your equipment isn't failing midgame, is it doing as much as it can for you? Too often, we don't think about tools we rely on because they work most of the time. Here's the thing, though: not every piece of hardware is created equal, and just because it isn't broken doesn't mean it's the best choice for you. Mice, mouse pads, keyboards, and headsets—each product comes with its own capabilities, and some of those are better for certain games and gamers than others. If you want to be the best, you need to make sure you have the right tools for the job. (Keep in mind that without a stable, high-speed connection, your fancy hardware will go to waste in online games.)

There's a lot to consider when picking the right tool for the job, and every choice is an opportunity to be the best player you can be. Ultimately, you're going to have to choose what works for you. But that doesn't mean the decision is simple, or automatic. Sometimes there really is a "best" piece of hardware. But most of the time, there are only ones that are "right" and "wrong" for you and your needs. To navigate this gray area, I want to help you really consider why you use what you use, and what you could be using instead. Your goal is to be more intentional about your choices and help you see the choices you didn't even realize you were making. Don't just fall back on the default or copy someone—even me! Now, let's *Gear Up*.

WHY YOU NEED A MECHANICAL KEYBOARD

· · · · ·

HOT 🔥 FIX!

You might be tempted by wireless keyboards—but don't be. Not only are they way more expensive and need regular charging, but they have slightly more latency than a mechanical keyboard. In a tight match, every advantage counts.

When you're just getting started with gaming, any old kind of keyboard can work. But if you want to get serious about playing well, then it's time to get a *mechanical keyboard*. What's the difference between that and a *membrane keyboard*? There are a few distinctions, but the big one is that your average USB keyboard has a single membrane inside it that's in charge of outputting signals to the computer. It works fine most of the time, but the signals can sometimes get muddled when the keyboard has to send a bunch at once. Input overflow means typos (if you're typing) or false keypresses (if you're gaming).

Mechanical keyboards solve this by putting each key on its own "switch." That way, there's no chance for the signals to get muddled—and when you're playing an intense game, a single false keypress can be the difference between victory and defeat. Unlike a membrane keyboard, a mechanical keyboard has a built-in feedback mechanism: the signature "click" that registers a successful keypress. Finally, mechanical

keyboards are a lot more reliable: a good key will last you 100 million clicks or more. Now, that's a lot of reloads! edits!

For all these reasons, mechanical keyboards are the best choice for gaming. But you still have plenty of choices to make. Full-size or half-size layout? What style of switches should you get? Let's walk through these.

GO FOR THE COMPACT KEYBOARD

· · · · · · · · · · · · · · · ·

Most mechanical keyboard manufacturers make both *full-size* and *compact* or *tenkeyless* keyboards. The main difference is that a full-size keyboard includes a number grid on the right side of the keyboard in addition to the alphabetical grid, whereas a compact or *tenkeyless* skips the number grid (get it?). The cons are obvious—fewer keys—but compact keyboards tend to be cheaper, take

KEYBOARDS AT A GLANCE

Note how many moving parts there are even in a single key of a mechanical keyboard. This gives you superior control and quality, but it comes at a cost.

With just one big membrane beneath the keys, you can see why a membrane keyboard is cheaper—but flimsier—than a mechanical one. Upgrade to a mechanical one as soon as you can.

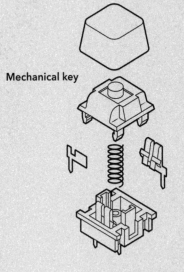

Mechanical key

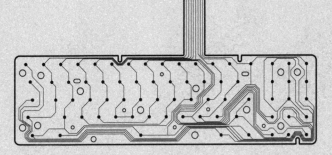

Keyboard membrane

FULL VS. HALF KEYBOARD

Think carefully before splurging on a full-size keyboard—you'd be surprised how little you'll miss those number keys when you're gaming!

Half-size

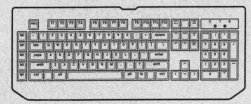

Full-size

up less space on your desk, are easier to transport, and are slightly more ergonomic. If you're really only going to be gaming, a compact one is often the better option. Since you'll have one hand on your mouse and another on WASD—your movement keys—chances are that you probably won't miss those number keys.

CUSTOMIZE YOUR KEYBOARD

One of the big advantages of mechanical keyboards is their customizability, especially with the switch mechanism. Different types of switches can adjust the volume of the "click" of a keypress (useful if you play in a shared space!), as well as the "actuation point," the amount of force needed to register a keypress. Some people like it harder, and some softer, but it's not just preference—check out the chart opposite to get a sense of your needs.

CHOOSING **MECHANICAL KEYBOARD SWITCHES**

Curious about the difference between red, black, and brown switches? It's subtle, but it mostly has to do with how much pressure you need to apply to a key in order for a keystroke to register—what's technically called actuation force. The exact amount varies from brand to brand, but black switches tend to require the most force, red the least, and brown somewhere in the middle. The drawback to a low actuation force, however, is that you're more likely to accidentally press a button. That's why fast, reflex-based games like first-person shooters benefit most from red switches, while other games with more elaborate keyboard layouts (MOBAs, MMOs, etc.) benefit from slightly more precise switches like brown and black. Ultimately, though, you should choose what feels most comfortable to you.

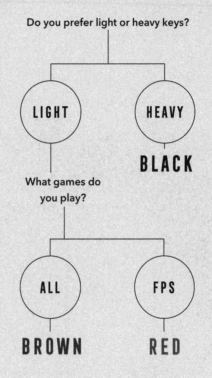

WHAT MAKES A GOOD MOUSE?

· · · · ·

A good mouse is one of the most important pieces of gear in any serious gamer's arsenal—it's the tip of your spear, and you want it to be as sharp as possible. That's why mouse accuracy is arguably the most important mechanical skill any gamer can develop, no matter what genre they're into. But to really master mouse accuracy, you need to be extremely comfortable with your mouse. And that means knowing how mice work, and the options that are available to you. Even with something as simple as a mouse, there's a lot to consider!

INVEST IN A GAMING MOUSE

················

Every mouse has what's called a CMOS sensor (aka "complementary metal-oxide semiconductor") that takes thousands of pictures each second. A tiny onboard computer compares these images to one another to determine the distance the mouse has traveled, which it then communicates to the computer. While you could use any old mouse to play computer games, you'll want to get an actual gaming mouse if you want to play your best—brands like Razer, SteelSeries, and Logitech make good ones. That's because, unlike the mouse that gets shipped with a basic office computer, gaming mice are built to endure years of heavy use, have better sensors that stay accurate even at high speeds, and can adjust their settings on the fly based on your needs.

Gaming mice are built to endure years of heavy use, have better sensors that stay accurate even at high speeds, and can adjust their settings on the fly based on your needs.

ADJUST YOUR DPI TO SUIT YOUR GAME

One of the advantages of gaming mice is that you can adjust your DPI—that's dots per (square) inch, meaning how many pixels your cursor can move when you move your mouse one inch—based on your specific needs. Many mice even let you do it just by pressing a button on the mouse! That's important, because different games have different optimal mouse settings. Take *Counter-Strike*, or any shooter game. Pros in these games tend to use a low DPI (around 800 or less) and low sensitivity, which lets them have more control over their movements. That way, if you need to turn your character around quickly or do a *flick shot* (more on that in Chapter 2!), you can whip your arm across the mouse pad. But if you need to make smaller adjustments, you only have to move your wrist.

WHEN TO GET A MACRO MOUSE

If you're into MOBAs (multiplayer online battle arenas) like *League of Legends* or MMOs (massively multiplayer online) like *World of Warcraft*, you might consider getting a mouse like Razer's Naga Trinity,

which has a side panel you can swap out if you need extra buttons. These mice let you map those skills to extra buttons, letting you control everything your character needs to do using the mouse, as well as the keyboard.

▶ **TIP** A macro mouse can be useful if you're playing games like *League of Legends* or *World of Warcraft*, in which characters have lots of abilities to manage.

GO FOR THE WIRED MOUSE

Not only are they cheaper, but wired mice have better in-game performance as well. Wireless mice have input lags of anywhere from eight to sixteen milliseconds—and while that might not sound like much, it can make a difference at very high levels of play, especially in games where reaction time is crucial.

With that said, wireless mice can be useful, too, in the right circumstances. If you're going to be doing some casual console gaming on your couch, a wireless mouse (and a laptop pad) can be a helpful ally. Just remember to keep it charged— there's nothing more frustrating than waiting for your mouse to charge when you'd rather be playing!

Gaming Mice Myths: Busted?!

Log on to any gaming forum, and you'll find people arguing about hardware, especially mice. Let's take a look at some common myths and separate fact from fiction.

Myth: **Optical Mice Are Better Than Laser Mice**

This one's half true. Optical mice are better in most situations, but a laser mouse is really just one kind of optical mouse. Both types use the same CMOS (complementary metal-oxide semiconductor) sensors, but laser mice illuminate whatever surface they're on using a laser (duh) instead of infrared or LED light. Lasers are so accurate that they actually respond to the *material* itself, and not just the distance the sensor travels, which can be a problem if you're on a soft surface like a gaming mouse pad. Since most gamers have a dedicated mouse pad (see page 22), mice optical sensors are the better choice.

Myth: **Higher DPI Is Better**

False! While it might seem like higher DPI means a mouse is superior, the truth is the DPI of most gaming mice is overkill.

Myth: **Your Mouse Sensitivity in Windows Should Be Set to 6 out of 11**

Also false! For a long time, this was true—your mouse sensitivity in Windows also determined in-game sensitivity, and setting it at 6/11 was the best way to ensure that data from your mouse was represented accurately on-screen. But pretty much every game made since 2000 uses "raw" or "direct" input, meaning that they bypass the Windows sensitivity setting in favor of their sensitivity. So focus your attention on in-game settings, not Windows!

DON'T IGNORE YOUR MOUSE PAD

• • • • •

Because they're so simple (or seem like it), mouse pads often get overlooked. But they're a crucial part of your setup because they bring out the best in your mouse, letting you make more accurate and smoother movements. That fancy, high-end Razer isn't going to do as much for you if it's on an old, frayed pad. Mouse pads might not have as many moving parts as mice, but there are still a few things to consider.

If you like to play a lot of different genres, it's best to go big.

SETTLE ON A HARD OR SOFT PAD

Soft pads are usually made of a synthetic cloth top and a rubberized bottom that keeps them from slipping. Hard ones are usually made from plastic and can provide an even smoother base for your mouse that requires less movement on your part, which some professional players, especially in aim-centric games like *Counter-Strike*, prefer. That said, you can roll up a soft pad and take it to your friend's place, but it's a little less convenient to do that with a hard pad.

SELECT THE RIGHT SIZE

Remember when we talked about DPI and mice? Well, that's relevant here, too. If your game is going to require you to make big arm movements (like many shooters do), you're going to need a big mouse pad that can support those movements. But if you're into MOBAs, strategy games, or MMOs, you can get away with a smaller pad. If you like to play a lot of different genres, it's best to go big.

GAMES VS.
MOUSE PAD SIZE

Picking the right mouse pad means weighing a number of different factors:
What kinds of games do you play? Do you want versatility or specialization? How much desk space do you have? What's your budget? Remember, even if you order online you can (and should) try a pad for yourself at a physical retailer.

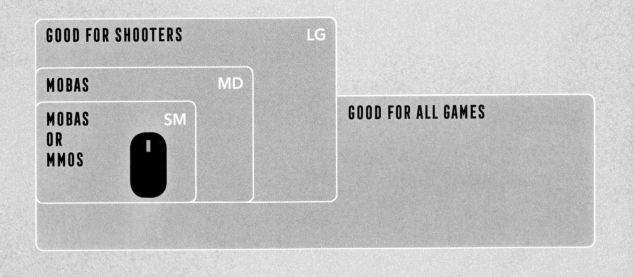

GOOD FOR SHOOTERS — LG

MOBAS — MD

MOBAS OR MMOS — SM

GOOD FOR ALL GAMES

HOW TO GET THE RIGHT HARDWARE FOR ANY BUDGET

· · · · ·

Now that we've talked about the hardware outside of your computer, we can take a closer look at what's inside it. Every gaming computer is built from the same set of parts: a central processing unit, a video card, a hard drive, a motherboard, and random access memory. You can always get a prebuilt one from a company like CyberPowerPC, Letsbld, or iBuyPower, but I strongly recommend building your own—not only because it's cheaper, but because you'll also learn a lot about the technology that makes gaming possible. You'll also be better prepared to troubleshoot any problems on your own.

WHAT MAKES A MONITOR "GOOD"?

. . . . .

For obvious reasons, monitors are a critical part of your setup, so it's worth springing for a high-quality one when you're able to. As with all the other hardware we've discussed, a number of things should be considered. Size, refresh rate, and resolution are the most important ones, but, most of all, you have to match your monitor to your hardware. If you don't, you're just wasting money.

HOT 🔥 FIX!

The "best" combination of hardware—where price meets performance—changes so often that it's not worth trying to list one here. Instead, you'll want to reference frequently updated online sites to determine the right gaming PC for you. Logical Increments (www.logicalincrements .com) is updated monthly to list the most cost-effective build—from a few hundred dollars to a few thousand.

A BIGGER SCREEN ISN'T ALWAYS A BETTER ONE

Gaming monitors tend to fall anywhere from 21 inches (measured diagonally) to 27 inches. While it might be tempting to go bigger (we all love a huge flat-screen television), the increased screen size means that you'll need to sit farther back for an optimal viewing angle. If you're gaming at your desk, sitting back far enough can present some serious logistical challenges, in addition to hurting your ergonomics. So stick with something in the 21- to 27-inch range. That said, if you're aiming toward the higher end of that, it's better to spring for a higher-resolution monitor. 1080P at 27 inches can look stretched, especially if you're used to playing games in 4K.

DON'T LET YOUR RESOLUTION EXCEED WHAT YOUR HARDWARE CAN DO

Almost every gaming monitor comes in one of three sizes: 1080P ("Full HD"), 1440P ("QHD"), or 2160P ("UHD," or "4K"). More resolution means more pixels, which means a sharper image. That can definitely help you get ahead in-game, but it also means that your all-important frames per second will suffer—the extra resolution is never worth it

Most Common Mistakes People Make When Selecting Hardware

Skimping on the Video Card

In almost all circumstances, the video card, and not the processor or any other component, is going to be the limiting factor for your computer. An excellent processor with a mediocre video card won't have overall performance better than a mediocre processor and a mediocre video card, so your GPU (graphics processing unit) is where the majority of your budget should go. And it's not uncommon to spend close to half the price of your computer on that alone.

Spending Too Much on the CPU

CPUs (central processing units) are massively powerful these days, and most serious processors have lots of extra cores to really crunch those numbers. But many game engines aren't even set up to take advantage of extra cores, so you're often wasting money on processing power you won't get to use! That said, if you plan on streaming or making your own videos, those extra cores can make a big difference. Be sure you do your research before you buy!

Getting Too Much RAM

For most users, 8 GB is all the RAM (random access memory) you'll ever need. Getting more RAM does not necessarily mean better performance. If a program can utilize only 4 GB of RAM, it's going to utilize 4 GB of RAM whether or not you have 4, 8, or 16 GB of it. Relatively few games are designed to use more than 8 GB of RAM at once—though that will probably change in the future—so unless you're going to do lots of video editing, anything above that isn't going to do you much good. If you really want to spend extra money on RAM, spend it on faster RAM, not more of it.

Not Checking Compatibility

Not all hardware is compatible with all other hardware. An Intel processor won't work with a motherboard designed for AMD chips, for example. There's nothing more frustrating than realizing that the nice piece of gear you just bought won't work with your computer. To save time and money, use a tool such as PC Part Picker (pcpartpicker.com) to check that each of your components is ready to play nice with one another.

if your video feed is stuttering. Keep in mind that the number of pixels your computer has to render increases exponentially (not linearly) as screen resolutions increase, which means playing in 1440P or 2160P place *much* larger burdens on your GPU.

AIM FOR THE HIGHEST REFRESH RATE YOU CAN

A refresh rate (measured in "hertz") is how many times a monitor can refresh its on-screen image per second. Most modern gaming monitors have one of three refresh rates: 60 Hz, 144 Hz, and 240 Hz. The higher the refresh rate, the smoother your game will be. In high-paced games like shooters, this means that you'll be able to see very fast-moving objects on-screen that might otherwise disappear "between" frames. The trade-off is that putting out more frames per second requires more powerful hardware, so there's no use getting a high refresh rate monitor if your computer can't handle it. Fortunately, the burden more FPS (frames per second) place on your GPU increases linearly, not exponentially, so it's easier to get the benefits of a high-refresh-rate monitor than a high-resolution one.

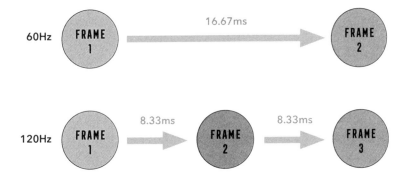

A GAMING HEADSET IS CRUCIAL

· · · ·

Communication is an essential part of competitive gaming, which means that your headset—your primary tool for hearing and being heard—is a vital part of your arsenal. If you can't speak, whether it's to teammates or practice partners, then you won't play your best. Period. You can always use the external speakers that came with your computer or a webcam microphone, of course, but the sound and recording quality are usually inferior and can disturb others around you (and vice versa). For that reason alone, a dedicated gaming headset is the way to go.

PICK YOUR HEADSET LIKE A PRO

You'll want to consider a couple of things when looking at gaming headsets:

- **COMFORT:** If a headset pinches your ears or falls off your head, then it's not right for you. Simple.

- **AUDIO QUALITY:** Have you ever put on a nice pair of headphones and listened to a song you like and heard something in it you never heard before? That's because higher-quality audio is crisper, and it's easier to make out individual sounds. When you're gaming, more information always makes for a better player.

- **BUILD QUALITY AND PRICE:** This is especially important if you think you're going to be using the headset in your day-to-day life, too. Like everything else, you want to hit the right balance of price and performance when buying a gaming headset. But if you're going to use your headphones at school or other places, you need to make sure you get a pair that's tough enough to be used every day. If the headset is just going to sit at your computer desk, strong materials—metal or thick plastic—aren't as important.

- **WIRED:** While you can go wireless, many of the same points made earlier with wireless mice and keyboards (pages 14 and 20), such as battery power, latency, and convenience, still apply.

  As with other hardware, it's always worth trying out headsets in person before you buy online.

BE PURPOSEFUL ABOUT YOUR HARDWARE

In the spaces below, write down the name of each piece of hardware and mark each piece of relevant information. Then, for each part, write one or two sentences about why you chose a certain piece of hardware, even if it's just "I don't have money for a better one yet." The goal is to make you reflect on your gear and be as intentional as you can about what you're using!

KEYBOARD [Mechanical vs. Membrane, Wired vs. Wireless, Switches, Size]

MOUSE [Wired vs. Wireless, DPI, Type]

MOUSE PAD [Hard vs. Soft, Size]

MONITOR [Size, Refresh Rate, Resolution]

HEADSET

ARM YOUR BATTLE- STATION

• • • • •

Since you're going to be spending a lot of time at your battlestation, it's important to make it as ergonomic as possible. This means designing an environment that helps you assume an optimal posture at all times. By posture, I mean the arrangement of your body in relation to the positions and movements you do throughout the day. That might sound obvious, but it's tougher than it seems. Try taking a short video of yourself while you play—do you look comfortable? Is your back straight, or are you hunched over your keyboard?

Your equipment is an important part of the ergonomic puzzle. You don't want to have to stretch for your mouse or keyboard, for example—if you're doing that, you're not going to be able to play your best. You'll also tire yourself out faster, and maybe even put yourself at risk of injury! Being intentional about where you place your peripherals goes a long way toward helping you sit in a healthy way. Doing it right will help you play longer (and better).

NINJA'S WAY

WHAT'S IN MY BATTLESTATION
I update my hardware every few months, but here's what I'm playing on right now—it easily runs *Fortnite* at 180 frames per second. Jealous? ;)

CASE: NZXT H700I
with Custom Ninja Wrap

CPU: Intel Core i9-9900K
8-Core 3.6 GHZ

CPU COOLER: NZKT Kraken X72

GPU EVGA Geforce RTX
2080 TI XC Gaming

RAM: Team T-Force Xcalibur
RGB 4000MGZ

SSD: Samsung 970 EVO

HDD: Seagate Barracuda 4TB

NZXT E850 Gold Digital PSU

HOW TO BUILD A COMFORTABLE SETUP

Let's take a moment to think about something that's directly connected to your setup: ergonomics, the science of arranging workplaces to best suit the people who use them.

PUT YOUR MONITOR AT EYE LEVEL

When you're sitting upright, your eye level should be at roughly equal height with the upper part of your monitor. Your monitor itself should be slightly tilted back and away from you. Position the center of your monitor below horizontal eye level, so you limit the amount of strain on your neck. You want to spend most of your time looking slightly down instead of looking up, which is tougher on your body. Not only will this allow you to play for longer without discomfort, it will ultimately be better for your long-term gaming health!

SIT ONE ARM'S LENGTH FROM THE MONITOR

Your monitor should be around one arm's length away from your body, give or take the size of your hand. Once you feel like you have your monitor in a good place, go ahead and adjust all your settings to maximize visibility and readability.

GET A DESK THAT ACCOMMODATES YOUR BODY

The correct desk height is one that allows you to do all of the above. It needs to be high enough that you can fit your knees under it comfortably, but low enough that your arms are parallel to the ground when they're on your mouse or keyboard.

FIND THE RIGHT CHAIR HEIGHT

The right chair height is one in which your hips and knees are even, and your feet are flat on the floor. When your knees and hips aren't even, your lower spine is pushed out of alignment to compensate, which can lead to back pain. Ideally, you'll have an adjustable gaming chair, but if you don't, don't be afraid to sit on a book or cushion. Likewise, your chair's armrests should be roughly the same height as your keyboard.

My Gaming Lair

After I blew up on Twitch in 2017, Jessica and I started looking for a new place for us to live. One of the first things I told her was "when I'm streaming, I don't want to be anywhere but the basement." For a long time, when we were living in apartments, I would use a spare room or just the corner of another room. But if I could have my setup anywhere, it'd be in a basement. When I lived with my parents, that's where I played. It's where I feel most at home when I'm streaming. So when we toured

what is now our current house, we saw this huge open basement and that's how we knew it would be ours. It was this large open space just for entertainment—there had been some kids living in the house before, and when we looked at it for the first time, there was still a Wii and some random games lying around.

But we knew it couldn't just be any streaming room—it had to be mine. Fortunately, Red Bull wanted to help us turn the room into something amazing that would really reflect my brand. So for the first few weeks we were living in the new house, I streamed from another part of the basement while a crew worked on what would become my streaming area. The whole setup ended up being finished while I was at TwitchCon. We didn't know at first if it was going to be ready by the time I got back, but the team from Red Bull managed to get it done about an hour before I arrived. I instantly loved it—my first stream after I returned home was just showing it off. I've got lots of cameras, blue and yellow lighting, a disco ball, a huge television I can analyze replays on, and, of course, a Halo sword and all my awards and trophies.

As cool as my streaming lair is, Jessica and I see it as a work in progress. The room is going to grow with us as I keep streaming. But whatever happens to it, it's always going to reflect something about who I am and what I'm trying to achieve.

WARM-UP EXERCISES

The truth is that competitive gaming is a physically demanding activity.

Gamers take a lot of heat for not being active, but the truth is that competitive gaming is a physically demanding activity. Keeping your body in good shape in both big and little ways will help you be the best gamer you can. Here are a few sketches that can help.

Even with the best ergonomics, gaming can take a toll on your wrists. In the short term, that can lead to tightness and discomfort, which will prevent you from playing your best. Over the years, however, it can lead to nasty problems like carpal tunnel syndrome, the "cure" for which involves spending a few weeks away from your keyboard! To avoid that, take a minute or two each hour to do a wrist exercise—before it starts hurting!

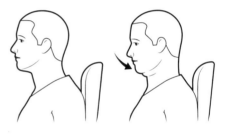

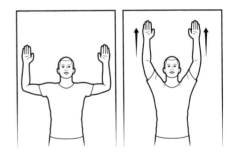

FOR SLUMPED SHOULDERS

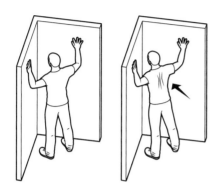

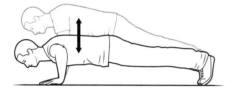

FOR SORE WRISTS

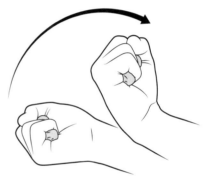

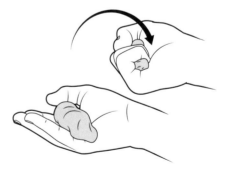

What makes a gamer great? Is it about being the best at one game—or all of them? Personally, I'm partial to the latter. **I want to be the best in everything I play, and I love taking on a new game and establishing dominance.** I didn't start with *Fortnite*, after all. My career has taken me from *Halo* to *H1Z1* to *Apex Legends* because I know how to adapt. And the truth is, there are core gaming skills that help you out in every game. Let's learn them.

In this chapter, I'm going to try to map out what I think are the main components of individual skill in games I love to play. It's not the only possible way of thinking about skill, and maybe you'll make adjustments to it as you improve and learn new things. But it's a starting point. And you should know that I'm going to focus on shooting games because that's what I'm best at. We're not going to get into too much detail about specific games, because mastering quick edits in *Fortnite* isn't going to help you land melee attacks in *Halo* and I want this book to be as useful to as many gamers as possible. But shooting games have some basic principles—like aim, movement, vision, and communication—that are relevant across a lot of different games. If you master them in one, you're going to have a much easier time transitioning to a new game, and you can spend the time you save learning what's unique about that specific game.

In this chapter, I'm going to start with clear, tangible skills—like mechanics, including aim and movement, and tactics; that is, decision making and game sense—for single-player games. Later in the book, I'll talk about teamplay skills (Chapter 4) as well as more abstract ideas like your mental state and overall attitude (see Chapter 6). For the sake of writing about them, I've had to put all these skills in isolation for the moment. But remember that skill, in practice, is holistic and complicated. It's really like a big knot. You can't separate decision making from mechanical skills, because if you don't think you have the mechanical skills to pull off a win in a certain fight, then that needs to be part of your thinking process. And, obviously, raw game knowledge impacts every part of skill. But even so: if you start to think about skill as a kind of *system* with lots of moving pieces, you'll start to see how it's more than the sum of its parts. But we still have to start with the parts.

BUILDING MECHANICAL SKILLS

• • • • •

Mechanical skills are your bread and butter, and they're what transfer most between shooting-based games. Good aim is good aim, and good movement is good movement, no matter what shooter you're playing. At the same time, good aim isn't just about mouse accuracy (though mouse accuracy is obviously an important component of mechanics, just like physical conditioning in basketball training helps with dribbling). It's a combination of game knowledge and mousework, and how the two work together.

MASTERING AIM

CROSSHAIR PLACEMENT

Ranged weapons in FPS (first-person shooter) games come in one of two types: *hitscan* or *projectile*. There's some very complex mathematical stuff going on beneath the surface, but the important thing for you to know is that hitscan means instant travel time and no bullet drop, while projectile weapons *usually* have a travel time and *usually* follow an arc, rather than a straight line.

Hitscan isn't all that realistic, but game designers often use it because it feels very smooth and players can easily see the relationship between cause and effect— wherever your crosshair is will be where your bullet lands.

On the other hand, projectile weapons, like the name suggests, have both a travel time and follow an arc. Projectile weapons are a lot more realistic, and so you'll see them in games like *PlayerUnknown's Battlegrounds*, which strive for lifelike accuracy. On the other hand, it makes aiming more skill intensive because you can't just point and shoot.

LEARN WHAT TYPE OF AIM YOU NEED

While aim might seem as simple as "point and shoot," it's actually a bit more complicated than that. There are different types of aim, and you need to understand which one is appropriate for what circumstances. The two most common types are *flick aim* and *tracking aim*, but we'll also talk about preshooting.

◄ **PREVIOUS PAGE:** Playing *Fortnite* with Mario Hezonja of the New York Knicks.

UNDERSTAND **THE WEAPONS IN YOUR GAME**

Most games these days have a combination of hitscan and projectile weapons. In *Fortnite*, for example, everything is hitscan except for sniper rifles, which are projectile. In *Apex Legends*, on the other hand, everything (for now!) is projectile except for the Havoc assault rifle. That means you need to know the type of gun you're using and plan accordingly. If it's hitscan, then just point and shoot. If it's projectile, aim slightly above whatever you want to hit. The farther the target, the higher above it you need to aim. Likewise, since the bullet's travel time isn't instant, if your target is in motion, you have to shoot where you think they're going to be.

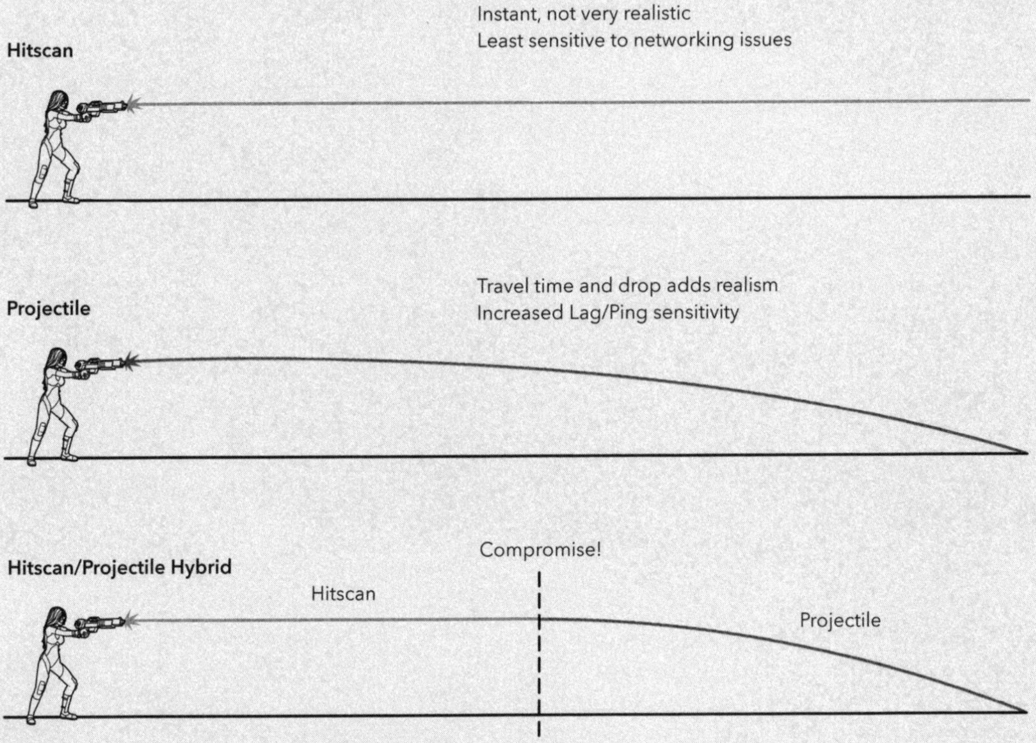

Hitscan

Instant, not very realistic
Least sensitive to networking issues

Projectile

Travel time and drop adds realism
Increased Lag/Ping sensitivity

Hitscan/Projectile Hybrid

Compromise!

Hitscan

Projectile

Flick Aim Lets You Get the First Shot Off

Flick aim, like the name suggests, is a lightning-fast reaction where you jerk your cursor toward a target (the "flick") and shoot as quickly as possible. Because it's a reaction, you're almost always responding to something when you're using flick aim, rather than trying to pull off a setup shot. Flick aim can be either defensive (flicking at someone who tries to surprise you) or offensive (getting the jump on someone); it's the rapid speed and wrist motion that define flick aim.

Since it's a reaction, or even a reflex, flick aim isn't something you think about so much as it's something you *just do*. That means you have to train your muscle memory until your flick shots are almost subconscious. When I do a flick shot, it's almost pure reflex, which frees up my mind to think about bigger strategic concerns.

HOT 🔥 FIX!

One of the most common errors I see people make has to do with preshooting. Often, when a player is heading over the top of a hill, they'll aim their gun upward because that's where they were aiming while they were walking up the hill. This makes intuitive sense: you want to see where you're going and shoot at anyone who comes over a hill when you're climbing up it. But it means that if you head over the hill and don't move your cursor, you're going to be aiming up into the air and not where your opponents are (on the ground). So try to get in the habit of aiming downward right *before* you go over the top of a hill, rather than right after. That way, if there are any enemies, you'll see them right away and won't have to move your mouse as far to get a clean shot off.

Use Tracking Aim to Take Down a Moving Target

Tracking aim, by contrast, means you're aiming and shooting at a target over time, rather than just flicking at them. Your objective with this kind of aim is to keep your crosshair on top of your opponent (or above and ahead of them if you have a projectile weapon) for as long as you can in order to get as many accurate shots off as possible.

In general, weapons with a high rate of fire (such as submachine guns [SMGs] and assault rifles) are going to emphasize your tracking aim, while ones that have a lower rate of fire (rifles and some pistols) are *usually* going to benefit more from flicks (as always, context matters!). That's not to say you're never going to flick aim with an SMG, because sometimes, you can and should. Likewise, tracking aim can be useful for snipers because you can keep your crosshair on a target while you wait for the right moment to shoot. Knowing which kind of aim is right for the situation is an important part of being a good player.

Preshooting Wins Fights Against Defensive Positions

The last main aiming technique is preshooting (sometimes called prefiring), which involves "lining up" a shot before you actually see your target. You can do this if you know where an opponent is, or likely to be. It's easiest to see in the game *Counter-Strike*, where preshooting is an important part of elite play.

There are only so many places on a map for opponents to hide, so if you know one of those spots is just around the corner, you can try to "line up" your crosshair in advance. That way, when you walk around a corner and get eyes on an enemy, you only have to move and shoot, rather than move, aim, and shoot. This will reduce the amount of time an opponent has to react to you, giving you a significant advantage.

HOT 🔥 FIX!

Let's say you get the jump on an opponent. What's the best way to maximize that advantage? One way is to attack them using what's sometimes called *movement aim*. The idea is that, if you manage to get your crosshair on an opponent before they see you, you can mimic their movements, rather than using tracking aim once they react to your attacks. If you can successfully mimic their movement, you'll keep them in your sights without ever having to move your mouse. This won't work in every circumstance, especially against very skilled players who know how to move erratically, but it's one way to reduce the complexity of your attack, making it easier to hit more shots.

Common Gaming Myths: Busted!

The more you get into gaming, the more you're going to be called upon to talk about, explain, or straight-up defend your hobby.

Even now, it happens to me all the time. When I talk to journalists or media personalities, they often ask questions about what kinds of effects video games are having on kids. Unfortunately, these aren't going away any time soon, so you might as well get used to responding to them. Here are a few of the most common ones, and what you can say if someone asks.

Violence

Pretty much for as long as video games have been around, people have been blaming them for all sorts of social problems. But nothing has been more consistent than the idea that video games cause violence. Psychologists and media experts have done literally thousands of studies on this and have never found a causal link between video games and violent behavior. In fact, the American Psychological Association released a statement in 2015 calling on politicians to stop blaming video games for violence.

Social Isolation

Another common fear is that video games make kids antisocial, or prevent them from developing good social skills. But if you've ever watched my stream or played *Fortnite* for yourself, you know that the opposite is true. Playing and watching games can be very social, and video games are a great way to meet new people or deepen your friendships with people you already know. In fact, one study found that people who identified as gamers were *more* likely to belong to some kind of social club, like a soccer team or a church group. Games are a great way to make new connections and deepen old ones.

Bad for School

Parents love to talk about how video games are bad for school. And, sure—if all you ever do is play video games, it's going to impact other parts of your life. But that's true of every activity, and there's nothing uniquely bad about video games when it comes to school. In fact, a lot of good research suggests gaming improves things like eyesight, concentration, and memory. Plus, a lot of the basic ideas behind this book—how to improve, how to be a good teammate—will help you throughout your life, including school.

Gamers competing at 2018 Red Bull Rise Till Dawn in Chicago.

MASTER GOOD MOVEMENT TO MAKE GREAT SHOTS

....

Everyone wants to be able to pull off killer headshots right away. But even if you have the best aim in the world, it's no good if you're not in the right place at the right time. Movement might not be the most glamorous gaming skill out there, but spending just a few minutes reviewing the basics of good movement in shooting games can lead to an *aha!* moment that'll pay off down the line.

You can boil down movement into one of two types: prepared or hasty. In a *prepared move*, you're moving on your own terms and in line with your greater strategy. As this is proactive movement, you should have a good idea of where you're going and why, and what you expect to find along the way.

The reality is that games are complex, we get taken by surprise, and even the best-laid plans run into problems.

Ideally, we'd all be doing prepared moves all the time, and, if you have an effective overall strategy, you'll be focusing on prepared moves most of the time. But the reality is that games are complex, we get taken by surprise, and even the best-laid plans run into problems. When that happens, we have to make a *hasty move*. Here, you won't have all the information but you have to move anyway, whether because you're getting shot at or there's an environmental hazard.

Finally, there's the business of staying still. Most of the time, you want to keep moving—if you're exposed, standing still makes you an easy target. But there are other times when it's worth it to stay still. Especially in battle royale games, it's often better to lie low and wait for an enemy to come to you, or for a more powerful group to pass by. Remember that, for some games, you may incur a penalty to aim if you're shooting while you're moving—so you always have to evaluate the benefits of staying still against the risks of moving (and vice versa). The only time you should really move while shooting is if you're assaulting someone directly.

HOT 🔥 FIX!

The best piece of advice I can give to you when it comes to understanding how aiming and mouse sensitivity work together is to start low, then go high. Begin with low sensitivity settings and get used to them—you'll have to make big movements with your arm instead of just your wrist, but it'll become more intuitive with practice. Once you're really good with that sensitivity, keep playing until you die during a fight because your sensitivity was too low. Now that you know what it feels like for your sensitivity to be too low, go ahead and up the sensitivity a little. Repeat until you find you're no longer losing fights because of your sensitivity settings.

OUTPLAY YOUR ENEMIES WITH SHOULDER PEEK

Shoulder peeking is a small, but important, technique. Using your strafe keys, you "peek" out from behind the wall to gain information (or sometimes to try to get a shot of your own) without exposing yourself to enemy fire. A good peek lasts less than a second, so use that time to figure out where your opponent is and how you might approach them, whether it's a direct attack (rarely a good idea) or trying to flank them (much smarter).

SECURE A HIGH-GROUND ADVANTAGE

Everyone who has played an FPS game knows that having the high ground is a serious advantage, but sometimes people struggle to articulate what actually is advantageous about it. The biggest thing is simply information: when you're higher up, you can see more, and that gives you a significant advantage over low ground opponents, who have less information than you. Having the high ground also helps with aiming projectile weapons. Since you're shooting down already, there will be less of an arc to the projectile, making it easier to predict where your bullet is going to go.

High-ground advantage comes in one of two forms: slope or absolute. A *slope advantage* just means that someone will have to walk up a hill to get to your position, but you still get all the vision and aiming benefits I just described. With an *absolute advantage*, though, there's no obvious way for your opponent to get to you. That means they either have to run away, or, if they're going to attack you, take a predictable path, which means you know where they'll be, giving you a chance to set up an attack.

STANDARD FIRST-PERSON SHOOTER **KEY BINDINGS**

Key bindings refer to your control scheme—what physical keys correspond to what in-game actions. While there are always some variations from game to game, virtually every first- or third-person shooter uses WASD as its standard control scheme.

    Remember that movement is a *combination* of actions by your right and left hand. Your left hand (on WASD) controls your position in digital space through strafing (horizontal movements) and forward/backward movement, while your right hand (your mouse hand) controls what direction you're looking. Usually, you're going to be using both hands together to get around in three-dimensional space, since you'll be looking in the direction you want to go. But sometimes it's useful just to move with WASD because it allows you to sidestep incoming projectiles without turning away from whatever you're looking at. If you watch a lot of battle royale streams, for example, you'll often see good players moving quickly from side to side using A and D while they loot defeated enemies' inventories. This also allows you to run away from an opponent without turning your back to them.

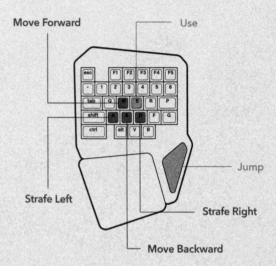

Move Forward   Use

Strafe Left

Jump

Strafe Right

Move Backward

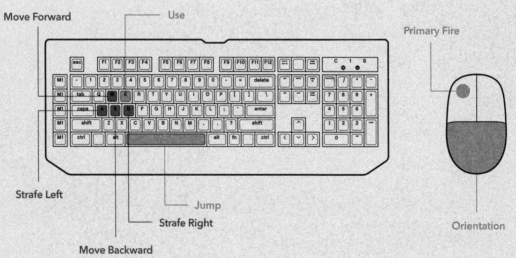

Move Forward   Use

Primary Fire

Strafe Left

Jump

Strafe Right

Move Backward

Orientation

WHAT GOOD MOVEMENT LOOKS LIKE

Watch a full match of me playing *Fortnite* and take notes on my movement. How often am I moving on my own terms (i.e., making a prepared move), and how often am I reacting to something else when I (hastily) move? For the prepared move, try to figure out what my intention was. For hasty moves, take note not only of what forced me to move, but also how I reacted to the threat and tried to gain control over the situation so that I could start making prepared moves again. Also ask yourself: What am I looking at when I move? Why?

Now do the same for one of your own replays, if your game has a replay function or if you're making video recordings of your own games (see pages 112-15). Try to figure out what you intended each prepared move to do—explain it out loud to yourself, or write it down—and, for hasty moves, figure out if whatever made you move was avoidable.

NOTES ON MAKING PREPARED MOVES

NOTES ON REACTIONARY MOVES

WHAT DO I LOOK AT WHEN MOVING

Settings as Strategy

In-game settings are another place to build an incremental advantage. Don't just try to max out your video settings, or stick with the default ones. Take a few moments to consider the possibilities.

Lowering the Resolution

If you have a 1080P monitor—that's 1920 x 1080 pixels—one thing you can try is telling the game to output video at a *lower* setting than that, which the monitor will then stretch to fit the screen. First, the pros: the lower resolution means that everything will look a little bit closer, which will make enemies easier to spot and, depending on the game, maybe even give them slightly larger hitboxes. (Plus, you'll get a nice boost in frames per second.) That's especially useful if you're still working at improving your aim.

There are some cons, though. Beyond making everything on-screen a little less appealing to look at, the stretched resolution means that your field of view is going to suffer, meaning that you'll see less of your environment at once. As a result, you'll need to strategize accordingly. The reduced FOV matters more in some games than others, so think carefully about whether or not you want to play with stretched resolution.

Tweaking the Graphical Settings

This is very game-specific. If you're playing just for fun, you probably like to turn up the graphics settings on your game as high as they can go (or at least as much as your computer can handle). But these settings are an important decision in their own right, and they can have a serious effect on in-game actions.

For instance, in *Fortnite*, if you turn the grass off, it may help you spot enemies in the grass more easily. Likewise, serious *StarCraft II* players often fiddle with their settings to make sure invisible units are easier to spot, or the screen stays clear of dead units. Death animations and persistent corpses look cool, but they add a lot of clutter to the screen and can be visually distracting and keep you from seeing what units are still alive (either yours or your opponents').

Ultimately, frames per second comes first—if you're dropping frames, you're going to be at a serious disadvantage against an opponent who isn't. But these kinds of tweaks can help create small edges over your opponents that you can exploit. Always take a moment to see what the pros are doing—if everyone seems to be using the same setting for something, that's a surefire sign that they have a reason for doing so. If you can't tell what that reason is, look it up or just ask!

DECISION MAKING

· · · · ·

In shooting games, you're always making decisions, whether you realize it or not. Where your gun is pointed, how you're moving and why—there's plenty to consider in every second of the game. I talked about some of these in the last sections, but here are other critical decision points for shooters.

ANTICIPATE FIGHTING

Just as there are hasty and prepared fights, there are also fights we're ready for and fights we're not. In a perfect world, we'd always enter fights on our own terms, so great players are going to do everything they can to move fights from the hasty column to the prepared column. This means knowing the map—where the hot spots for fights are, for example—and knowing your opponent. If you have a good sense of when a fight is going to go down, you can make the decisions you need to put it on your terms. Remember, if you're going into a fair fight, then you haven't been preparing enough to give yourself an advantage.

TURN A LOSING FIGHT INTO A WIN

It's pretty much human nature that, if someone thinks they're about to win a fight, they'll drop their guard and go in for the kill. In doing so, they often overextend themselves, creating an opportunity for a counterattack. This happens all the time in games—if you're retreating from a fight, chances are that your opponent is coming after you because they think they've already won. Their greed creates opportunities for you. While retreating is sometimes the right call, always look for opportunities to reengage on your own terms. You'd be surprised at how often you can turn a losing fight into an even one, or even an outright win.

Remember, if you're going into a fair fight, then you haven't been preparing enough to give yourself an advantage.

DEVELOPING GAME SENSE

· · · · · ·

People sometimes act like game sense—the ability to know what's happening or about to happen in a game—is mysterious. And maybe some people just naturally have better game sense than others, but the best way to get game sense is to practice and take notes. The more you've seen, the easier it is to guess what's going to happen next. Just like training flick aim can become muscle memory, building game sense can transform predictions you have to *think* about into intuitions you just *feel*.

Building game
sense can transform
predictions you have
to *think* about into
intuitions you just *feel*.

NINJA's WAY

" **MY GAME SENSE** Game sense can be a little abstract, so let me give you an example of what it feels like. Let's say I'm playing *Fortnite*. I glide into Retail Row from the south. I see two people fighting, so now I know there are people in front of me. I hear a snipe to my right, so I know there's now someone to my east in addition to the two to my north.

The zone's moving in. I'm not safe, so I know I've got to run in thirty seconds and I just entered a build fight with the survivor from the fight that was in front of me. So I've got an internal clock—I know how quickly I either need to defeat this person and move out, or disengage now, while *also* making sure that I stay out of the line of fire from the sniper to the east and/or wall off that angle of attack during the build fight. Game sense means holding all that in your mind at once and letting it shape your decision making as you play. "

Taking in victory at the 2017 Halo Championship Series in Las Vegas.

My Biggest Win

The first major tournament I ever won was MLG Fall Championship 2012, back when I was playing *Halo* for the team Warriors. Obviously, that meant a lot to me, but the win that really sticks with me the most was the H1Z1 Invitational at TwitchCon 2015, which was the first major event I won on my own. Back then, I was having modest success as a streamer but nothing like today. And I was still really trying to make a name for myself on my own. So I was super nervous going into the competition, even though I'd practiced like fourteen hours a day in the weeks leading up to it—I'd never been in a real battle royale tournament before and I didn't know what to expect.

When the game started, I was terrified I'd be knocked out early until I found my guns and a vehicle. Then I calmed down, took stock of what was going on, and tried to play my game as best as I could. Once I got a kill, I allowed myself to start thinking that I could win it all if I played smart. I did, and I won—the winning moment is still up on my Instagram. I ripped my headset off and jumped up, yelling something I can't put in the book—pure joy. Winning $20,000 was nice, of course, but the feeling was priceless. All the practice was worth it. 100%.

So you want to be a professional gamer? Then get ready to work for it. If playing video games for a living were easy, everyone would do it. Fortunately, I've picked up some tricks along the way that you can use to accelerate the process of becoming the best player you can be. If the last chapter was about what makes a good player, then this one is about how to become one. The truth is, getting better at video games isn't all that much different from getting better at anything. It takes practice, obviously. But it also takes intention, patience, and planning. Just playing isn't practice, and it won't get you the results you want. So what will?

THINKING INSTRUMENTALLY

· · · · ·

In the first chapter, I encouraged you to take a step back and be intentional about all your hardware choices. This chapter is all about being intentional with how you approach *practice*, which is not the same as playing. It's how you turn playing into something more.

We're going to take stock of all the techniques you have to pull that off, and figure out how to put them to the best use. That means we're going to be thinking *instrumentally*—I want you to look at your own practice habits and rationally evaluate what you could be doing better. The hard truth is that the work of improving isn't always fun—or, at least, it's less fun than logging on for a few rounds with your friends. But champions win by creating—and exploiting— incremental advantages, so if you want to be the best, that's what you've got to learn. On their own, a lot of the things I'll describe can sound trivial. But put them all together, and it's the difference between being a good player and a great one. Let's get started.

FOUR PILLARS OF
IMPROVEMENT

KNOWLEDGE
Raw Knowledge About
Your Game. Numbers.
Locations. Names.

MECHANICS
The Fundamentals. Aim.
Movement.
Mouse Accuracy.

TACTICS
Game-Specific Actions.
Edits. Combos.
Slick Moves.

STRATEGY
Higher-Level Thinking.
Game Plan Decision Making.
The Big Picture.

KNOW WHY YOU WANT TO GET BETTER

• • • • •

This might sound like a silly question, but before we get into the weeds, it's worth asking yourself why you want to be great at games. Is it to show off to your friends? To try to win some money or get famous? Because someone told you you couldn't, and you want to prove them wrong? Or simply because you enjoy the feeling of mastery? Ultimately, there aren't right or wrong answers here—I think everyone should be free to play games for whatever reason they want.

But when it comes to *competitive* gaming, some reasons for improving *are* better than others. Talk to any professional gamer, and you'll be amazed at how few of them cared about getting rich or famous (at least at first). Great gamers are built upon their love for the games they play, and it's important to always keep that in mind. Just like musicians want to express themselves through their instruments, great gamers express themselves through competition, by exploring their games, pushing their limits, and discovering something about themselves in the process. Gaming has taught me so much about myself, and it can do that for you, too, if you let it.

NINJA'S WAY

" **DISCOVER YOUR COMPETITIVE INSTINCT** Every competitor has a moment when they stop playing just for fun. I was twelve years old when I wanted to be better than my brothers at *Halo 1*. And then *Halo 2* was when my competitive urge really kicked in. The ranking system came out and I wanted to rank higher than my brothers. So we would always play for fun, and then when they weren't home, I'd play without them and improve my ranking. Then we'd play together again, and they'd get crushed. At that point, I was, like, "All right, I'm better than them. I don't like losing. I'm going to keep playing my own game." And that's how I got started. "

WHAT SKILL IS MADE OF

• • • • • •

There's a lot that goes into playing well, and if we're going to split it up into manageable parts, we need to map out what skill looks like. Again, this isn't definitive—another professional gamer might split it up differently—but it's a tool to get us thinking about all the things that go into making a great gamer so that we can start to isolate specific areas for improvement.

HOT 🔥 FIX!

At some point, you've got to identify some specific skills and try to target them. Just like a soccer coach might instruct their players to do a corner kick drill in practice, you should try to break the game down into specific skills and find ways to practice them. But there's a dark side to repetition. Use practice to reinforce only good habits. Bad habits will have to be unlearned and then relearned, creating more work for you down the line. That's why it's so important to isolate the skill you want to work on, and then review.

ACQUIRE RAW KNOWLEDGE

....

How much damage does each weapon cause? What's the damage spread? Projectile speed? How many bullets are in a clip? Where are certain power-ups (beneficial objects or abilities) located? How much mana (or any other resource) does a particular ability use? What's its range? How long does it take to walk, run, ride, or fly from one point to another? Obviously, there's a lot to learn about any given game—watch any professional gamer on Twitch and, chances are, you'll catch them learning something new about their game. But as intimidating as the task is, mastering this information is a crucial part in becoming the best player you can be.

Challenge yourself to know everything you can know, because every bit of knowledge you have that your opponent doesn't is an opportunity to create and exploit an advantage. Seagull—one of the most famous players in *Overwatch*—once told *Rolling Stone* a story about how he started preparing for the game even before he had access to the beta. "I made spreadsheets of all the damage numbers I could find," he said. "I wrote strategies for maps I hadn't even played by looking at three- to four-minute gameplay previews on Blizzard's YouTube channel. I tried to track the internal balance patches to see how the designers viewed the game and what direction they wanted to take it. I wrote ten thousand words on *Overwatch* before I touched it." That work put Seagull at the front of the *Overwatch* scene when it launched. Are you willing to do the same for your game?

HOW MUCH DO YOU REALLY KNOW?

Without looking, write down as many weapons or heroes from your game as you can, as well as their relevant attributes (damage, clip size, stats, abilities, etc.). I promise it's harder than you think! Doing so will give you a sense of what you still need to learn.

"COUNTER YOUR OPPONENT'S STRATEGY Just like rock, paper, scissors, pretty much every well-designed video game makes space for "counters" against whatever the most powerful strategies are. Just as "rock beats scissors," a counter simply means that a certain item, ability, tactic, or strategy will disrupt another strategy, reducing its effectiveness. If you want to be a top player, you need to have this knowledge down. Knowing how to recognize your opponent's strategy, and use an effective counter, is an essential part of a good player's skill set.

Good in-game analysts often distinguish between "hard" and soft" counters.

- *Hard counters* deliberately and completely shut down one or more parts of your opponent's game plan. For example, in *Dota 2* the Butterfly item gives its user the ability to evade a percentage of attacks but is hard-countered by Monkey King Bar, which ignores evasion, rendering Butterfly almost useless.

- *Soft counters* negatively impact an opponent's strategy and tip the odds in your favor, but don't necessarily guarantee a victory on their own. If you're playing *Overwatch*, you can pick defensive heroes to delay an enemy push, but you still have to execute well to get the W.**"**

PRACTICE YOUR MECHANICS AND PHYSICAL SKILLS

Just like dribbling in basketball or soccer, there are some gaming skills that are a "given" in a great player, so you need to practice these building blocks till they're basically second nature to you. Do you think LeBron James thinks about dribbling when he's on the court? Of course not, but he manages to dribble nearly perfectly every game. Pulling that off takes muscle memory, which can come only from practice. That'll help you avoid silly mistakes, but, more important, it'll free up your mental energy to focus on other, higher-order tasks we'll talk about in the next few pages.

Mechanics include mouse control, left-right hand coordination, eye movement, and their corresponding in-game actions, like aim, movement, and camera control. Simply put, these are second nature to me and I can trust that, if an enemy is on-screen, I'm going to be able to quickly and accurately get my cursor over them. Obviously, different games have different mechanics—good movement in shooters won't help you much in *League of Legends*—but they're still pretty consistent within genres, which is why I was able to transition from *Halo* to *H1Z1* to *Fortnite* without too much trouble. Mouse accuracy, for obvious reasons, is going to help you out no matter what game you play.

IMPROVE **MOUSE SKILLS** WITH *OSU!*

What's the best way to improve mouse accuracy? Obviously, the more you play, the more comfortable you'll get with understanding how your hand movements match your cursor's (or crosshair's) on-screen motion. Still, there's a couple of tools out there that you can use to accelerate the process. A lot of professional gamers use the (free!) rhythm game *Osu!* to train and improve their mouse

accuracy, or just to warm up before tournaments. It's basically *Dance Dance Revolution* for your mouse hand. The music might be obnoxious, and the colors are admittedly pretty annoying, but it'll train you to click accurately and get your hand motion and mouse clicks in time with each other. It starts easy, but its higher-difficulty settings will test just how precise your mousework can be.

TACTICS AND STRATEGY

"Strategy without tactics is the slowest route to victory. Tactics without strategy is the noise before defeat."

—Sun Tzu, *The Art of War*

Sun Tzu's quote is a classic distinction made by military planners, but you'll find that it's also applicable in gaming. The chart on pages 68–69 shows some of the main differences, but the gist of how I think about it is this: tactics are the actual set of actions you perform to reach

a certain goal, while strategy is your overall plan to reach that goal. For example: If you're playing *Dota 2*, you might have a *push strategy* but your actual *tactics* involve grouping up with your entire team and attacking enemy towers. Tactics and strategy are yin and yang—there's always a bit of overlap between them, and they don't make much sense without each other. But they're a useful tool for thinking about your approach to your game.

GET YOUR HEAD AROUND TACTICS

Tactics, unlike mechanics, tend to be game-specific. It's a bit reductive, but you can think of it as the place where mechanics and knowledge come together to produce particular actions. As a simple example, let's say I'm playing *Fortnite*, I'm in a building, and I know there's someone coming up the stairs behind me. A low-risk tactic for me is to drop a trap on the stairs, which will either do a ton of damage (or outright eliminate them) or force them to go another way, both

	STRATEGY	TACTIC
WHAT	Overall game plan comprised of multiple tactics	Tasks, formulas, and policies for getting stuff done
WHERE	The "big picture"	Localized
WHEN	Long or medium term	Immediate
HOW	Planning where to deploy armies to win the war	Running in a zigzag to dodge enemy fire

of which can be put to my advantage. Now, a single trap is too local of an action to be a strategy—you probably shouldn't base your entire game plan around traps (but if you can pull it off, I want to see how you do)—but it is a combination of knowing what the right tool for the job is and where it should go.

DEVELOP A STRATEGY. REFINE IT. REPEAT.

Here's where the high-level thinking kicks in. As I talked about in Chapter 2, strategy is all about putting yourself in the most advantageous position (and, by extension, your opponent in the most disadvantageous position) possible. If you're in a fair fight, you're not being as strategic as you could be.

Remember that attention is a finite resource, just like ammo or health. You want to put most of your thinking into strategy, but you can only do that if you've mastered the "lower" tiers of skill. For example, when I'm playing a shooting game, I'm not expending mental energy trying to get a headshot. Rather, because I can trust my mechanics—that is, my mouse accuracy and aim—I can spend that mental energy on setting up opportunities for me to get the shot I need.

▶ **TIP** Your mechanics won't do you any good if you can't set up chances to use them! When you're competing at a high level, it's never enough just to outplay your opponents. You need to outthink them, too—that's the art of strategy.

STRATEGY—DOING THE RIGHT THING

	EFFECTIVELY	INEFFECTIVELY
EFFECTIVELY	**WIN QUICKLY** A good plan done well	**LOSE QUICKLY** A bad plan done well
INEFFECTIVELY	**WIN SLOWLY** A good plan done poorly	**LOSE SLOWLY** A bad plan done poorly

DOING THINGS RIGHT

ISOLATE SKILLS

When I was younger, I would rage whenever I got killed by someone better than me. And the only thing I understood about getting better was just putting in more practice hours. Now I have the intelligence to be, like, "Hey, I'm lacking in this area and I'm going to go practice this skill offstream for thirty minutes." I learned to isolate skills and practice them, which is one of the most important parts of improving.

One of the big challenges—probably the biggest one—of gaming well is that you have to manage all these aspects of skill (knowledge, mechanics, tactics, and strategy) at once, in addition to communicating with your teammates if you have any. No one—*no one*—has the ability to improve every single aspect of their play at once. You will, of course, get better *in general* by playing, but that can only get you so far—think of all the people you know who have played two thousand hours of a game and didn't seem to improve at all after their first couple of hundred hours.

Repetition isn't just about building muscle memory—it's also about establishing familiarity with a skill. Just as you can instantly recognize when your friend gets a haircut, knowing what something normally looks, feels, or sounds like lets you know when something is different. That principle is very useful in gaming. Let's say you're playing *Smash Ultimate*. If you play ten matches with ten different heroes against ten different opponents, chances are you're not going to repeat the same scenario more than once, which means it'll be hard to recognize it and learn the best response to it. But if you play ten matches with one character against one opponent, you reduce the variables in play and you can isolate what's powerful—or not—about your character.

TREAT PLAY AS PRACTICE

If you're serious about getting better, you need to set up a schedule, not just by setting aside a slot of time for dedicated practice, but also having a plan for what to do with that practice time. Warm-up, free play, drills, replay review, scrimmage—you need to make space for all of it.

SET UP A PRACTICE SCHEDULE. STICK TO IT.

You'd be amazed how much your perception of gaming changes when you start taking it seriously. When you give yourself a schedule and stick to it, playing stops feeling like just play. Instead, that time starts to feel purposeful. At that point, you should begin to see results.

TO SKILL UP, DRILL DOWN

Pick one game you want to improve at. Write down as many skills as you can think of for that game. Then pick one skill, open up your game, and play a match with that ability in mind. Devote all your attention to that skill, whatever it is, even to the detriment of other ones (just for now, obviously). Chances are you won't win because you're deliberately tunnel visioning on one skill—that's okay, because learning, not winning, is the point of this exercise.

By repeating the exercise, the skill will become muscle memory and you won't have to spend as much mental energy on doing it well. As it becomes more natural, you can start focusing on another skill—repeat the cycle as many times as needed.

HOW LONG SHOULD YOU PRACTICE?

Maybe you're tempted to practice ten hours a day right out of the gate. I like your enthusiasm—hold on to that—but the truth is that practicing like it's your job probably isn't going to serve you well at first. If you're really serious about getting better, you need to start slow. Put aside an hour or two a day to practice seriously. You should be prepared to face the possibility that you simply won't enjoy this kind of work—and there's no shame in that! If you don't, it's better to get your feet wet before you dive in only to discover that you'd rather just play casually.

▶ **TIP** A good practice session involves playing a match, reviewing it, taking notes, doing a drill, and playing another match to see if you can improve on whatever you think your biggest weakness was. See page 74 for a sample session.

As a general rule, the better you get, the more you can and should practice. As you grow in skill, you'll want to spend more time with your game, mastering its intricacies, and internalizing its mechanics. Not only will you get better at the game; you'll also get better at practicing the game, accelerating your improvement.

◀ **PREVIOUS PAGES:** Pro tennis player Taylor Fritz and Kevin Knox of the New York Knicks playing *Fortnite* in L.A. while I was in town for the ESPYs.

NINJA'S WAY

" MY IDEAL PRACTICE PARTNERS
Because I mostly played team shooters, I didn't have a lot of one-on-one practice partners—that's more of a thing for 1v1 (one versus one) games like *StarCraft* or *Smash Bros.*, or things like practicing a lane matchup in MOBAs. But we still had teams we'd play against and the idea's pretty similar—you have to find the person or team who's your kryptonite. Who are you losing to? Play against them over and over and over and over again.

I always tried to get the person or team who you're, like, "I don't understand why they do what they do." I think about Hungrybox in Smash—in my opinion, he'd be the greatest practice partner in *Smash Melee* because everyone hates his playstyle. He sucks to play against! But that makes him an amazing player to learn how to play against. Mang0, on the other hand, is one of the best players in the game, but he's also superrandom. He's a wild card, and do you really want to practice against someone who is so inconsistent? Even *he* doesn't know what he's going to do when he starts a game. He just goes crazy. **"**

PRACTICE PLANNING; PLAN PRACTICE

If you've ever been to a sports practice, you know that good coaches don't just have you scrimmage the whole time. They are going to divide up the time effectively and build a kind of teaching strategy in which the practice builds on itself. It's a good model for thinking about your practice, too. Start with the little skills, work up to something bigger, and then take a second to reflect on what you've learned.

You can use the basic formula below for practice sessions that last anywhere from one to a few hours, depending on how long each practice game is or how much time you have.

WARM-UP

Play a match. Have fun, but use it to get into your practice headspace. Remember: you're not just playing, you're working, too. And take a minute or two to stretch (see page 36). You'll be glad you did.

SKILLS

Identify a skill you need to get better at (movement, aim, building, etc.), ideally something you know you're struggling with from past review sessions. Figure out how to isolate it, or do some drills using an online aiming tool (there are plenty out there, so just google until you find one you like). Repeat the drill until you start to see what you're doing well, and where you can improve. Write that down.

SCRIMMAGE

Play a real game, and try to keep whatever skill you were practicing in the front of your mind. No matter what happens, devote time and mental energy to doing that skill as well as you can so you can see how it translates to real games.

REPLAY

Whether you won or lost, take a second to review the match if you can (see page 51). Can you say with certainty why you won, or why you lost? What are the areas for improvement? Be sure to write these down—not only will you better commit them to memory, but they're also a useful resource for thinking about what you're going to target in your next practice session.

Adjust how much time you spend on each section according to your needs. It doesn't have to be perfectly even. When you take practice seriously, you'll be amazed at how quickly you'll start seeing its effects in real games.

DON'T RISK BURNOUT

There's a limit to how much practice pays off. Good practice is hard work; your mind will get tired and you'll also risk burning yourself out. Ultimately, a lot of research shows that you stop really benefiting from additional practice after about *six hours a day*. So until you're a professional, consider that your hard limit. You can play more than that if you want—stream, goof off, play casual matches, and so on—but know that the chances that you're going to get more than six hours of "good practice" out of one day is pretty low.

FIND PRACTICE PARTNERS

One of the fastest ways to improve your skill is to get a practice partner. There are plenty of benefits to practicing with someone. One is accountability—when I'm practicing on my own, there's no one but me to stop me from goofing around. If you have a practice partner, though, you've got someone to hold you accountable and keep you on task. Likewise, with a practice partner, you can specify what skills you want to work on. Maybe you want to master a certain area of the map, get better at a specific matchup, or focus on a certain tactic. Like playing catch with a friend, practicing with or against someone is a great way to work on your fundamentals in a somewhat more controlled environment.

FIND LIKE-MINDED GAMERS

Not all practice partners are created equal. The right practice partner isn't necessarily someone who is much better than you, or much worse than you. The practice partner you want is someone who is committed to getting better *with* you—someone who also sees practice as more than just playing, someone who is willing to put improving skills first, someone who won't get tilted when they're struggling. It's great if you can find someone in your IRL (in real life) friend group who is as serious about a game as you are. For example, both Kevin "PPMD" Nanney and Adam "Armada" Lindgren, two of the best (retired) *Super Smash Bros. Melee* players in the world, practiced almost exclusively with their brothers throughout their careers.

Of course, that's not always possible. Online forums are a great spot to look for similarly skilled, similarly minded players. You can even meet people in-game, like players you were matched with and enjoyed talking to. Just remember that it's important to find someone with the same mentality as you. You should avoid toxic players—if someone berates you or another player, just move on. It's not worth spending time with someone who is going to be emotionally exhausting when you're trying to become the best player you can be.

HIGHER- AND LOWER-SKILL PRACTICE PARTNERS

Sometimes you'll hear people say that the only way to get better is to play with people better than you. There's some truth to that—if you don't challenge yourself, there's only so much you can improve. Playing against people who are better than you will help you see the parts of your game that you can improve. If you're losing because your opponents are picking you off from behind, then you need to work on your positioning and map awareness. If you're getting into 1v1s but can never manage to eliminate your foe first, then you need to work on your aim and reflexes. What's more, a truly excellent—and truly generous—player may be willing to mentor you, pointing out what you're not doing well and accelerating your rate of improvement.

But consider the flip side: it's not enough to know why you're losing—you also want to know why you're *winning*. Getting the W isn't just a matter of making fewer mistakes, but also recognizing and exploiting your opponents' errors to build an incremental advantage. To do that, you also need to play against players who are *worse* than you. That way, you can see common errors, faulty strategies, and the best way to respond to them to make sure that you come out on top.

Streaming in Paris with my buddy Gotaga, who even taught me a little French.

HELP A PLAYER OUT

When people agree to practice with you, they're doing you a favor—so pay it forward. Every time you ask someone to drill a certain skill with you, you should be prepared to drill whatever they want to work on, too. And when you get good, remember that you, too, were a less-skilled player once. Help new players, and show them the tools of the trade. Teaching others isn't just a nice thing to do. It's also one of the best ways to make sure you understand things as well as you think you do.

RESOURCES FOR GROWTH

Even without a practice partner, there are still a lot of resources at your disposal to help identify and work on the things you're struggling with.

WATCH REPLAYS LIKE YOU MEAN IT

While it's not as fun as actually playing, watching replays is a key part of getting better. It's very hard to be conscious, in the moment, of every decision you're making. But remember: when you're gaming, you're always making decisions, even if they're not ones you're aware you're making. Replays are useful for figuring out what you might have done differently, or seeing your play with new eyes to assess why you're losing.

MAKE USE OF TWITCH AND YOUTUBE

One of the most amazing things about today's internet is the sheer volume of content out there that's designed to help you get better. You're not alone in wanting to get better, and a huge and constantly evolving amount of resources is out there to help you improve. Search for a *Fortnite* tutorial on YouTube, and you'll find countless videos that explore the island, show you where all the best loot spots are, explain various mechanics, and test different weapons. Watching these can save you a ton of time and frustration. Why do work that someone else has already done for you?

Just like real practice is never *just* playing, not all watching is created equal. Some streamers will commentate their gameplay, which is an excellent way to get tips and tricks from people who are more highly skilled than you. But even if a streamer isn't commentating their gameplay, you can still get a lot of knowledge by watching closely. Take notes. Write down what they do well—and what they don't. Watch streamers of all levels. Figure out what kinds of things separate the good from the great, and then try to emulate them in your own play.

BUILD SKILLS WITH FREE-PLAY MODES

Free-play modes are useful because they can let you try out certain skills, without the pressure of losing or being reported by your teammates. These days, most games include some kind of "free-play" mode. *Dota 2*, for example, lets you control everything using console commands, from levels, to health, to items. *Fortnite* has its "creative" mode. What's more, these modes often give you tools to create very specific situations that don't come up very often in "real games" but are important to respond to nonetheless. Use that freedom to build your knowledge and skills. Even now, I'll hop into *Fortnite*'s "playground" mode to practice building skills in a low-pressure environment for thirty or forty-five minutes before I get onstream.

NINJA'S WAY

WHAT I LOOK FOR IN REPLAYS

I usually never watch games that I win because you learn a lot more from losing than winning. So if I watch a replay, it'll be because I got smacked. And I tell myself, *All right, I need to watch what this person did and how they built.* Sometimes there's just not much you can do—if I'm playing *Halo* and I'm playing with randos but get crushed by a professional team, there's not much to say. But if it's a close game, that's where you gotta take a step back and watch the replay. Those games are usually decided by one play, and that's what you've got to look for: the play that lost you the game. And you have to watch it right away, when it's all fresh in your mind, or else you'll lose the details about how it felt. You'll forget why you did a certain move, like jumping or looking in a certain direction. Maybe you heard a snipe shot, maybe you thought you heard someone you thought was coming in and you can't see that in replay, so you need to make sure you remember those details.

STAY MOTIVATED

Getting better consists of two parts: hard work and motivation. If everything I've described here seems exhausting, it's because it is. If it feels like work, that's because it is. And, as with work, it's not always fun to do. If your mentality is just to push through, you're going to burn out eventually and forget why you loved playing games in the first place. That means staying motivated is *at least* as important as doing the hard work of improving. Never stop reminding yourself why you want to improve. Plot your progress. Save your best games, and look at them when you're discouraged. Remember the compliments you get. Give yourself rewards for hitting milestones. Share your achievements with your friends. The challenge isn't working hard to do hard work—it's finding the motivation to make hard work feel easy. Master that, and I promise there's nothing you can't do.

Streaming live at my event Ninja's Night Shift in Warsaw, Poland, where I competed against hundreds of amazing players.

NINJA'S WAY

HOW I STAY HUNGRY I know I'm not going to be the best at what I do forever. And I'm always the first to admit when someone is better than me, because it shows that I need to improve some aspect of my game. It's that drive that motivates me—the desire to always be better. Constant improvement in every single aspect of my life—for me, that's literally it. Just competitiveness. If you don't have that hunger to be better than someone, to put in the effort you need to be better than someone, then you're in the wrong line of work.

Staying motivated is *at least* as important as doing the hard work of improving. Never stop reminding yourself why you want to improve.

One Night in Vegas

Sometime ago one of the guys from Esports Arena flew out to Chicago and met with us to go over the vision for what we'd want to achieve with a Ninja-themed event in Las Vegas. It was their idea, but we took it from idea to reality together. We really wanted to make it about me as this new kind of gaming celebrity that flew in the face of any kind of negative stereotypes about gamers as sloppy or whatever. So that's what guided the design of the event. I got a carefully cut suit that looked amazing, because I wanted to walk onstage dressed to the nines and let everyone know what kind of event we were running. We also had drink service and catering to really round out the night.

Jessica actually worked as the host for the Vegas event, so it was amazing to get to do something like that with her. We obviously work closely together a lot of the time, but that was the first time we'd done anything like that. It was, as far as I know, the first event a streamer ever did on his own, so we really invented something new there. A lot of people think that my stream with Drake was the most concurrent viewers I ever had, but the Vegas event actually beat it out by quite a bit. But for all the hype, when I think about the most memorable moment of that night, I have to admit that, well, it was winning.

TEAM UP.

4

If you're serious about being a competitive gamer, chances are that you're going to play a team game. What that means for you is that learning how to be a good teammate is just as important a skill as being a good individual player. **You can be one of the highest individually skilled players in the world, but if you suck to be on a team with, your career isn't going anywhere.** That's why this section focuses on making you the best teammate you can be, and how working with others can help you achieve goals that you couldn't achieve alone. Let's team up.

Everyone wants to be the flashy star player, but the reality of competitive gaming is that you're going to shine only as much as your teammates let you. If you look closely at some of the best gamers in the world—pros like Faker, Arteezy, and Olofmeister—you realize that they're only able to style on their opponents the way they do because their teammates make them the space they need to shine. That goes for sports (and just about anything), too: even Michael Jordan wasn't *Michael effing Jordan* until he had an elite group of teammates who made it possible for him to play his best. And even if you're practicing a single-player game, you're still going to need coaches, practice partners, and analysts. As far as I can tell, the truth is that there really are no single-player games. No matter what you're playing, you can always do more together than you can on your own.

◀ **PREVIOUS:** Pulling an all-nighter will DrLupo at the 2018 Red Bull Rise Till Dawn in Chicago.

▲ **ABOVE:** DrLupo and I pose with the winners Nate Hill and SoaR Funkbomb of Team Exploit at the event.

WHAT MAKES A GOOD TEAMMATE

· · · · ·

NINJA'S WAY

" **RIVALS—FRIEND OR FOE?**
Personally, I try not to think about rivalries because I think it can divide communities. It drives fans apart because it forces them to choose between different streamers. Now, if a rivalry is superfriendly—like "who can do something positive first?"—or jokes around with me a lot, that's different. Having someone to compete against can help motivate both of you and drive attention on social media, but you have to make sure that it stays lighthearted. "

In Chapter 2, "Power Up," I said we'd come back to team skills. Obviously, your individual skills still matter, as do ideas about strategy and tactics. But there are other skills that are unique to playing on and as a team—like communication and team composition.

HOW TO BUILD A GOOD TEAM

· · · · · · · · · ·

The essence of a good team, like any good system, is that it's more than the sum of its parts. That's true both in-game and out of it. A truly effective squad isn't necessarily the one with the best players, but the one that uses the players it has to the greatest impact. The history of esports is filled with superteams that, on paper, should have been the best in the world but fell flat on their face when the time to compete arrived. Putting the right team together means knowing as much about what's going on outside of the game as you know about what's happening inside it.

Bottom Line: No matter what game you're playing, your team is a system, not just a couple people playing video games. That means picking heroes or champions whose abilities synergize effectively, or collecting an arsenal of weapons that complement one another. It's no good going into a gunfight if everyone has the same pistol—that just limits you. Always take a moment to take stock of what your team composition is, and think about how it could be more flexible.

STRATEGY AND TACTICS

Remember these? Strategy and tactics don't just matter in individual play—they're a key part of playing, training, and thinking well together.

PLAN A TEAM STRATEGY

The World War II general Eisenhower once said, "In preparing for battle, I've found that plans are worthless but planning indispensable." He's right—whatever your strategy going into a game is, chances are it's going to change, but it doesn't mean your team shouldn't have a strategy going in. If you take a few moments before the game just to define a style of play—defensive, mobile, hyperaggressive, passive, and so on—then you're going to be more organized than you would be otherwise. All those strategies can be good or bad in different contexts, but making sure your team has a common idea of what to do in cases where the "right" play isn't obvious will do wonders for making sure you're actually playing as a team.

Just having a shared mind-set will make you feel more like a team.

DEVELOP TACTICS TOGETHER

One way of thinking about team tactics is as a complex puzzle with a limited number of solutions, some better than others. Team fights are some of the most interesting and complex things a video game can offer because you have to think about so many variables. But good tactics means taking stock of your resources and the situation, and identifying the best "fix" to whatever mess you're in. In general, the best tactics are going to be proactive and force your opponents into making hard decisions where there aren't "good" solutions.

Celebrating with my old teammates on Luminosity at the 2017 Halo Championship Series, where we tied for fifth place.

COMMUNICATION IS A WEAPON, TOO

A silent team is a dead team. You need to be constantly communicating with your teammates about what you're seeing and your overall game plan. In a contest between two evenly matched squads, the one with better communication wins. So whether or not you're matched with randoms or playing with your friends, put your microphone to use. It's as much of a tool as your weapon, and if you wield it well, you're going to be in a better position to win.

That said, not all communication is created equal. You want to share as much information as you can, but you also don't want to confuse or distract teammates. Communication is a skill, and like all skills, you have to practice it. Stay cool, calm, and collected and relay the most information you can while trying to keep it simple. (See the Hot Fix! on page 143.)

In fact, all the things you don't say are just as important as the things you *do* say. You need to weigh the importance of what you're saying against the risk of saying anything at all (your teammates probably don't need to hear that you collected some extra ammo, unless, of course, there was an ammo shortage). That's easier in theory than practice—watch any professional game in person, and there's a good chance you'll see plenty of yelling over one another even in the most disciplined teams—but it's still something to aspire to.

COMBOS AND SETUPS

No matter what game you're playing, you're going to have to work as a team to pull off powerful combos or set up favorable engagements.

The term *combo* originally comes from fighting games, where it refers to a series of perfectly timed actions that make it nearly impossible for an opponent to do much of anything, but it's spread out to pretty much every video game. These days, a combo just means putting together two or more skills so that they have more impact than they would on their own—it's 2 + 2 = 5, in a sense. A simple example in *Overwatch* is when Zarya uses her ultimate, which holds enemies in place, and her teammates use area of effect abilities, like Hanzo's ultimate, on their trapped opponents.

Being able to pull off team combos is a hallmark element of elite play, but it requires a bit of coordination. If a certain combo requires your teammates to use abilities in a certain order, you can plan that order in advance. Alternatively, your shotcaller can yell out "three, two, one, go!" if you need to use your abilities simultaneously. Things won't always be that easy in a real match, though, so you might just have to tell your teammates what you're doing in the moment and hope they can respond. Coordinate in advance when you can, and let your teammates know what you're doing when you can't.

ADAPT, IMPROVISE, OVERCOME

Inevitably, based on what happens in a given match, you're going to need to alter your strategy, tactics, composition, and communication techniques. The role you have at the start of the game might not be the role you have at the end of it. While there's always a tension between general game skills and more specific kinds of expertise, when you're on a team, you need to recognize that there will be situations when your commitment to your specific "role" is dragging down the team (this is one of the biggest mistakes I see in amateur teams—tunnel visioning on your role and missing the bigger picture). Sometimes healers need to become damage dealers; sometimes aggressive characters need to play defensively. It's all about context. Listen to and trust your teammates, because that kind of flexibility and faith in one another is part of what separates good teams from great ones.

Here's a good example: just because you're your team's support player at the beginning of the game doesn't mean you won't ever be a primary damage dealer. A few years ago, Evil Geniuses, then one of the best *Dota 2* teams in the world, was playing a long game against one of their rivals. When it became clear early on that this would be a very long game, one of their support players switched from playing their hero in a support role to a damage-dealing one. As a result, Evil Geniuses' hero composition grew in strength as the game went on, and they eventually won because of it.

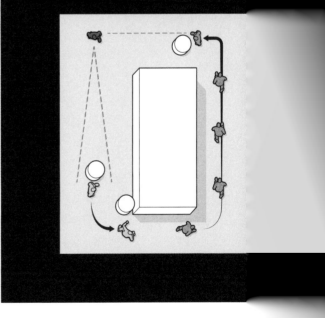

NINJA'S WAY

FLANKING MANEUVERS One of my favorite tactics is flanking. Here's how flanking maneuvers work. The "problem" is that one or more of you team members (maybe you) is pinne down by enemy direct fire. You coul try to run at enemies directly, but tha probably not the best solution since they'll be stationary and you won't be able to aim as well while you rusl them. Instead, a better firing solutior is having your teammate run around Here's how it works in action.

Team Tactics 101

Direct Fire

Bullets, basically. Direct fires are your classic, primary gun-based attacks. What's important here is to remember that these always follow a straight or close-to line and do damage at a specific point—not, say, area of effect—which has implications for when it's useful and when it's not.

Indirect Fire

Everything in your arsenal that isn't a gun? That's your indirect fire. Grenades, airstrikes, whatever. Unlike guns, these don't necessarily follow in a straight line. They might arc or bounce or be user guided, but regardless of their path, they give you different tactical options.

Combined Arms

Like the name suggests, using combined arms involves both direct and indirect fire to achieve a bigger goal. A simple example is throwing a grenade (indirect fire) to flush out an opponent who can then be shot (direct fire).

Concentric Fire

Concentric fire means that you have multiple people shooting at the same target. Good players can usually make the "right" choice when there's only one source of danger, but when there are multiple ones, even the best players can get confused and make hasty mistakes.

Suppressive/Covering Fire

Suppressive fire (sometimes called covering fire) is both tactical and psychological. Not only does it scare opponents and potentially force them into making a hasty decision, it can keep them in place and prevent them from firing while your teammates (or you) can move around with minimal risk.

Pins

Pinning means you've managed to corner your opponent in such a way that there's no way for them to escape without exposing themselves to direct fire.

LEADERSHIP

When you're playing as a team, it's often the case that someone is going to need to take on a leadership role. Call them captains or shotcallers, they're the people you look to for guidance in-game when things are crazy. You can probably guess that being a good leader is a skill, but it's also true that being a good follower takes practice as well. Let's consider both.

Posing with Gotaga (*left*) and Broken (*right*) while I was in Paris.

HOW TO LEAD

In team games, it's the shotcaller's responsibility to make sure that the team is working together as a unit: ideally, they make the decisions about when to be aggressive or be defensive. A great shotcaller isn't necessarily the player with the highest individual skill, but the one who sees the big picture. They aren't just focused on getting one kill, which might not actually matter much for the game as a whole. Instead, they see how that kill fits within a bigger game plan. They don't just make decisions based

on what's in front of them, but what's going to happen in thirty seconds, one minute, five minutes, or even ten minutes. A good shotcaller has that kind of expansive game sense. They don't micromanage; they steer the ship and trust the people they're commanding to do their jobs.

That said, whatever the benefits, being a shotcaller is stressful, just like all leadership positions. It requires responsibility, and you have to earn the trust and respect of your teammates, which takes a huge amount of experience and perspective that you build up over hundreds or thousands of hours of playtime. Inevitably, though, you're going to make a bad call at some point. And while it can be tempting to defend whatever choice you made in order to maintain your authority, sticking to a mistake is going to make you look less, not more, legitimate as a leader. Be open-minded, not arrogant. Learning to take constructive criticism seriously will help you become the kind of in-game leader that your teammates will want to follow.

HOW TO FOLLOW

It's a common misconception that damage dealers are the in-game leaders. In fact, you'll often find that that slayer, run-and-gun types make better followers than shotcallers. That's how it was in *Halo*, and it's often the case in MOBAs, too. That's because your damage dealers are like the tip of a spear—they might have the most firepower, but they have to be wielded by someone else. An effective follower listens to and acts on the order and

HOT 🔥 FIX!

In battle royale games, getting eyes on an enemy usually means that it's about to go down. If you've got the jump on your opponent, then it'll be a fight in your favor. But if they've got the jump on you, you need to get into cover and reset the fight. Either way, your teammates need to know.

When you're playing with other people, your first instinct when you see an opponent is probably to say something like "I see someone over there."

You're right to alert your teammates, obviously, but you're not really telling them much useful information. Where is the enemy? Are they coming toward your team, or going away? Do they seem aware? "Enemy by the forked tree" reveals much more information than "I see someone over there" even though it's fewer syllables.

Just like you should try to instrumentalize every aspect of your play, you should try to make your communication as intentional and efficient as possible. When you're playing with friends, try to convey as much information in as few words as possible. It'll take conscious effort at first, but, eventually, it'll become a habit.

information they get from their shotcaller so as to just make plays wherever they can. And a really effective follower will also say what they're doing so that the shotcaller can consider that as they continue to survey the battlefield.

When you're following orders, it's natural to occasionally doubt whether or not a command you were given was the right one for the situation. And it's totally okay to challenge your shotcaller's orders if you really think they missed something—that's how great teams improve, together. But you probably want to wait to do so until after a game is over to have that conversation. That way, you'll be a few steps removed from the heat of the moment and you'll be able to look at the replay together (if your game allows for that). Sometimes, it really is clear that one person was right about a call that didn't work out. But, most of the time, I find that both the shotcaller and whoever is challenging them each have good points based on their different perspectives. Good players will take that to heart, and keep it in mind the next time there's a questionable play.

NINJA'S WAY

" **DEFUSING TEAM TENSION** Back when I was playing competitive Halo, I got into an argument with my teammate Spartan (aka Tyler Ganza). He thought he had a great strategy, and I thought he was wrong. It got heated. So we took the conversation offline, away from the game, and talked about what we were trying to achieve, which ended up being the same thing by different routes. In the end, we were able to incorporate both our ideas once we saw that each of us had strengths and weaknesses. "

TO GET GOOD TEAMMATES, BE A GOOD TEAMMATE

• • • • •

Hopefully the last few pages have convinced you that playing well on a team requires a lot of skill. But that's only half the story. You need to also think about how you're going to be a good teammate *outside* of the game. There's a good chance you already know what this feels like in practice: think of the people you genuinely enjoy playing with. Chances are, they're good teammates. They don't take their frustration out on others, they know how to take constructive criticism, and they have the same goals as you, whether it's "have fun" or "get better." In short, a good teammate is someone you *want* to play with. And one of the best ways to attract good teammates is to be one yourself.

HOW TO DEFUSE
TEAM TENSION

· · · · · · · · · · · · · · · ·

If you're on a team of competitive gamers, things are going to get tense at some point. No one likes losing, and no one likes to make mistakes, but both are bound to happen when you're trying to be the best. And, chances are, when you make a silly mistake or lose an important match, you're going to feel like blaming one of your teammates. You're only human, after all. Maybe you think they made a bad call, committed an unforced error, or just aren't taking the game seriously enough. So what then?

Nothing kills a team faster than a toxic environment, so when tension arises—and I promise it will—you need to know how to defuse it as soon as possible. Prevention is best; try to talk out issues before they build up and become a serious problem. But when a real argument goes down, you can try to deal with it in a few ways.

Try to talk out issues before they build up and become a serious problem.

- A self-deprecating joke is a quick way to let your teammates know you're not really mad at them, and if they respond with another joke, things will be back to normal right away.

- Apologizing has that effect, too: even if you're not certain that you're in the wrong, apologizing and trying to move on is sometimes the most effective thing to do. Remember, being in a team is also about managing relationships, and it means that you sometimes need to do things that you wouldn't otherwise do.

- Change the subject. When things are tense and don't seem like they're going to get better with an apology or a joke, ask about literally anything else. Tell them about something you saw onstream. Ask what else they're playing. Get their heads away from a problem, and you can come back to it when everyone is a little more calm.

- Step away. Sometimes there's really nothing to do but log off. It's always okay to say, "Hey, this isn't productive, let's talk later" and do something else for a while. Good teammates will see the wisdom in that. By the time you get back, whether it's an hour or a day later, everyone will be in a better place to talk through whatever issues you're facing.

Rise Till Dawn

The Las Vegas event was such a success that
I knew we had to do a follow-up. Around
that time, my stream was really starting to
take off, so I wanted to do an event that paid
homage to competitive gaming's origins in
all-night LAN parties with your friends. But
Red Bull is always looking to do something
extreme, and when they came up with the
idea for doing an overnight event at the
top of the Willis Tower, the second-tallest
building in the US, I knew we had to do it,
because it kind of synthesized where I'd
come from and where I was now. And that's
how Red Bull Rise Till Dawn was born.

Fans came from all over the world to
take part in the event, which was basically
teams of two trying to get as many kills and
win as many *Fortnite* games as possible
in between 8:21 p.m., when the sun went
down, and 5:35 a.m., when the sun rose over
Lake Michigan. My teammate for the night
was DrLupo, which drove home the fact that
this was an event all about playing games
with your friends and doing things you could
never do alone.

I'm glad we did it, but the next morning
was rough. I didn't think we were going to
make it all night (thanks, Red Bull). When
we finished, Jessica and I went back to the
hotel—turns out you can't play video games
all night and be functional when you're not a
teenager anymore.

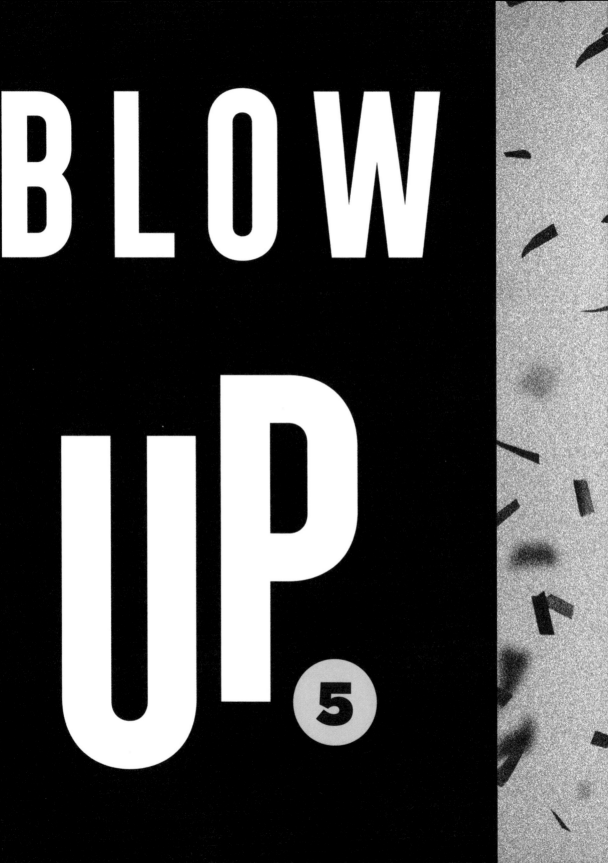

BLOW UP
5

So you've been practicing hard, you're pretty good at games, and you're ready to share your skills with the world. I can't blame you—it's hard for me to think of a better career than playing video games for a living. The catch is that a lot of other people think that, too: hundreds of thousands of people stream on Twitch *every day*. **How are you going to stand out in that crowded field?** How do you even get started with streaming? What are some important milestones to hit? In this chapter, I'm going to walk you through what makes a stream great—and how you turn private play into public entertainment.

Let's get something out of the way now: there are no guarantees in streaming. You can be the most charismatic person and the best player out there, but there's no direct path to becoming a streaming superstar. There's lots you can do to try to build a community, improve your content, and connect with your audience—and we'll talk about all that in this chapter—but an element of chance is always present. Take me, for example: I happened to get into *Fortnite* at the right time, and it meant that I blew up super quickly. If I had been a little earlier, or a little later, or picked a different game, it's possible you'd be reading someone else's book and not mine. I can't show you how to become the biggest streamer on Twitch, but I can show you how to make the most compelling stream you can. And remember: you don't have to blow up on Twitch for streaming to be worthwhile!

WHY SHOULD YOU STREAM?

NINJA'S WAY

STREAMING IS NETWORKING
No streamer is an island. I'm lucky to be surrounded by some of the coolest, most passionate people I know, and I owe as much of my stream's success to them as anything I've done myself. Streaming is networking, and, over time, you'll build up a network of friends on Twitch who can help make your content better than you could by yourself.

MEET PEOPLE

I can't tell you how many new friends I've made through Twitch. Streaming video games has connected me with amazing and passionate people around the world, like Tim (TheTatMan), DrLupo, and BasicallyIDoWrk. I've been a guest on their streams, and they've been guests on mine. Gaming is better with friends, and streaming is a great way to share your friendship with the world.

SHOW FRIENDS WHAT YOU'RE UP TO

While playing video games usually gets all the attention, people have been watching one another play video games as long as they've been around. These days, streaming is a great way to share your passions with the world, or even just your friends. Whether you're trying out a new game for the first time, or showing off your skills with one you've finally mastered, streaming gives you a new way to connect with your friends. At its best, it can really feel like your friends are in the room beside you, cheering you on (or maybe just taunting you a little—we all have that friend). Seeing one of my friends in chat and knowing that they're supporting me in doing what I love is an incredible feeling.

ACCOUNTABILITY

If you're trying to improve, having a scheduled streaming time is one way to help structure your time effectively. If you know there's someone waiting to watch you play, then it's a lot harder to let them down, which means you won't be letting yourself down, either. What's more, your audience can be your best, biggest critic—but in a good way! Even if you've got only a couple dozen viewers, that's still a couple dozen sets of eyeballs keeping an eye on your gameplay. They'll see mistakes, things you miss, and, if you ask them, they'll let you know. Sometimes, they might even know something you don't! Never let a resource go to waste.

Your audience can be your best, biggest critic—but in a good way!

MAKE A LITTLE MONEY

Of all the reasons to stream on Twitch (or wherever), this one is the least important. Chances are, if your metric for success on Twitch is getting rich, you're going to end up being disappointed. You *can*, of course, make money on Twitch—from ads, donations, subscriptions, sponsors, and channel games—but very few people earn enough to make full-time streaming viable, and they certainly don't do it right away. It took me years to get my audience where it is today, and even now, there are no guarantees. Games come and go, audiences change their minds, advertising rates go up and down, and life beyond your stream can throw you curveballs, too. So making money shouldn't be your goal when you start—it's something you work up to over a long time, and you have to accept that even if you do everything right, you might not ever make enough to be a full-time streamer. What's a lot more likely is that you'll get a dollar here and there from a generous viewer, and you take pleasure in knowing you've given them something that's worth it to them. That's a gift in itself.

Wait, *How* Popular Is Twitch?!

As of 2018, Twitch was one of the most popular websites on the entire internet. On any given day, more people watch Twitch than CNN.

560 BILLION
Minutes watched

3.7 MILLION
Broadcasters a month

1.3 MILLION
Average viewers at once

220,000
Twitch Affiliates

56,000
Average live channels

27,000
Twitch Partners

You can always look up the most current information at twitchtracker.com/statistics

WHAT DO I NEED TO STREAM?

· · · · ·

YOUR HARDWARE

Just like gaming has its own gear, there are a couple of things you'll need to get started with streaming. Inevitably, the hardware we have for streaming is going to change and improve over the next few years, so there's no use in listing specific products here since they'll soon go out of date. But I *can* say a few general words about the technology behind streaming. The truth is, streaming can be tough on a computer, especially if you're playing a graphically intensive game. If your computer is already struggling with

THE **BARE-BONES SETUP**

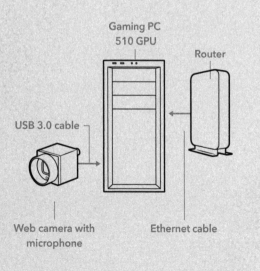

Gaming PC
510 GPU

Router

USB 3.0 cable

Web camera with
microphone

Ethernet cable

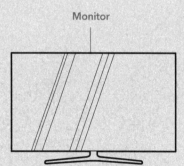

Monitor

graphically intensive games, there's no way it's going to be able to handle playing *and* streaming, which requires your video card to capture, encode, and upload a live feed of your gameplay to your streaming service. That means the better your hardware, the better your stream.

THE BARE-BONES SETUP

If you've got a gaming computer, there's a good chance you'll be able to make a respectable stream without any additional investments. There's nothing especially fancy about this setup, and so there are some obvious limitations. You won't be able to stream any game at 60 frames per second at 1080P (the gold standard as of 2019, but expect a lot more 4K streams soon), and your audio probably isn't going to be as sharp as what you'd see on professionals' channels. But your viewers will be able to see, hear, and understand you. It's a nice way to get started with streaming and build your skills and on-air personality without having to invest too much into the hardware.

THE **INTERMEDIATE SETUP**

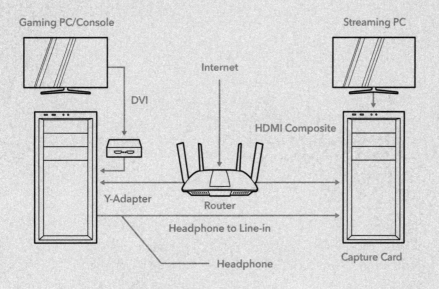

INTERMEDIATE SETUP

When you're ready to take streaming a little more seriously, it's time to enter the land of serious hobbyists. The big difference in this setup is that we're no longer relying on a single computer to do everything. Instead, we're distributing some of that responsibility to other pieces of hardware, some of which is built with streaming in mind. Most obviously, that means you'll have a separate PC for streaming with a capture card that's linked to your gaming PC. That in itself takes a huge amount of pressure off your gaming PC, and it lets you keep an eye on your stream with a second monitor. But that also means starting to invest in some dedicated hardware: leaving the webcam's microphone behind and getting a real USB microphone and maybe even a dedicated DSLR (digital single-lens reflex) camera in video mode, which will let you set up different angles and massively increase the quality of your video. For 95 percent of streamers, this is all you'll ever need.

THE ULTIMATE CONTENT CREATION WORKSTATION

This setup is *absolutely* overkill for streaming on Twitch, but I have to admit it's a lot of fun to look at just how complicated a setup can get for the most demanding users. The idea behind this system is maximum redundancy and flexibility. It gives you complete control over different camera views, in-game and

INTERNET

You can probably guess that having faster internet—especially your upload bandwidth—is going to make your stream better. Obviously, the more data you're putting out, the more bandwidth you're going to need. But unless you have a really serious streaming setup, you'll just want to set your streaming output for 30 frames per second. That means your resolution is the main thing you should consider when you're trying to figure out what your bandwidth can reasonably handle.

HD BROADCAST

1920×1080 (FULL HD)—MINIMUM 3.5 MBPS UPLOAD

1280×720 (720P HD)—MINIMUM 1.8 MBPS UPLOAD

720×480 (720P HD)—MINIMUM 1.2 MBPS UPLOAD

SD BROADCAST

720×480 (480I SD)—MINIMUM 350KBPS UPLOAD

320×240 (240I SD)—MINIMUM 200KBPS UPLOAD

THE **ULTIMATE CONTENT CREATION WORKSTATION**

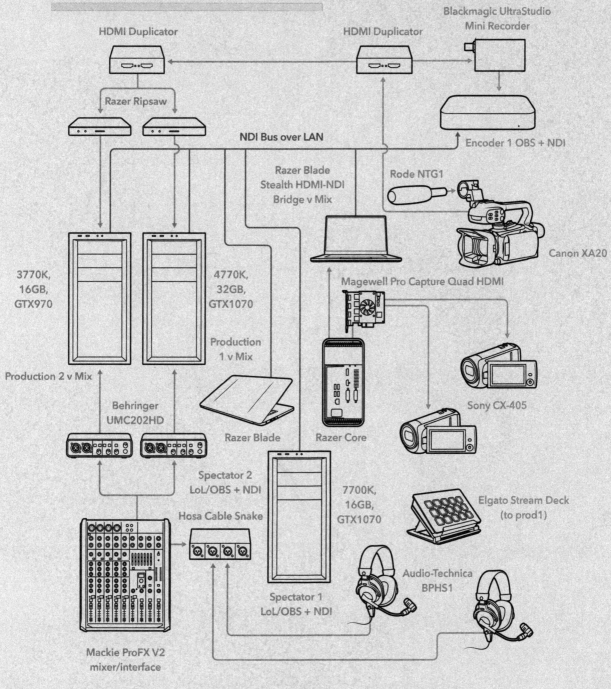

Blackmagic UltraStudio Mini Recorder

HDMI Duplicator

HDMI Duplicator

Razer Ripsaw

NDI Bus over LAN

Encoder 1 OBS + NDI

Razer Blade Stealth HDMI-NDI Bridge v Mix

Rode NTG1

Canon XA20

3770K, 16GB, GTX970

4770K, 32GB, GTX1070

Magewell Pro Capture Quad HDMI

Production 1 v Mix

Production 2 v Mix

Behringer UMC202HD

Sony CX-405

Razer Blade

Razer Core

Spectator 2 LoL/OBS + NDI

Hosa Cable Snake

7700K, 16GB, GTX1070

Elgato Stream Deck (to prod1)

Audio-Technica BPHS1

Spectator 1 LoL/OBS + NDI

Mackie ProFX V2 mixer/interface

Your Streaming Environment

No matter how much money you're putting into your streaming hardware, it's always worth taking a few minutes to think about your environment—that is, the space around your computer. Here, you've got two main choices, and as with most things, there are pros and cons to consider.

Green Screen

A lot of streamers like putting up a green screen—basically a big monochrome sheet—behind them. Because of the consistent color, your computer can easily cut out the background from your video feed (the fancy term for this is chroma key compositing), leaving only your body in the live video output to your stream. On-air, this looks very polished, and if you're streaming from a very messy space, it can make your stream look a lot cleaner. Plus, setting up and taking down the green screen is really easy, so it's especially useful if you don't have a dedicated space in which to stream. The downside is that it limits what you'll be able to show to your viewers, for better or worse—you won't get to show any fun stuff from your environment like posters, pets, friends walking by, or gear from sponsors. Just remember not to wear something green yourself!

Live Video

Your other option—the one that I use—is having a direct video feed of whatever room you're streaming in. Obviously, you'll want to make sure that you're in the frame—your viewers are there to watch you, after all—but you'll also want to consider what else will be sharing the frame. In my case, I have a dedicated room for streaming where I've been able to set everything up to my specifications. Think about what you can do to your environment to make it feel as professional as possible. You probably want it to be clean, and if there's a wall behind your chair, consider putting up some posters that let viewers know what you're passionate about. Having "real" space onstream is also an opportunity for product placement, which will be important if you ever get sponsored.

Lighting

It's always worth investing in a little bit of lighting for your setup—even a simple floodlight by your computer is better than just ambient light. You'd be surprised at how much more professional a stream looks when the streamer has taken the time to put a light on them, because it really focuses the viewer's attention on what matters—you!

out of it, ensures that there's never a hiccup during encoding or uploading, and backs almost everything up because the show must go on. In practice, this is the kind of content creation system used only by full-time, high-end video producers who do much more than just streaming.

THE SOFTWARE YOU NEED TO STREAM

Whether you've got a high-end streaming setup or something much simpler, you've got a lot of options for the kind of software you're going to use. Like everything else we've discussed, it's always worth taking a second to make sure you're using software that helps you acheive your goals.

WHAT'S A CAPTURE CARD?

A *capture card* is a great way to upgrade your game when you're ready to take your stream to the next level. When you've got two PCs at your disposal—one to game on, and one to stream—the capture card is what makes them work with each other. The graphics card in the gaming computer continuously sends data to the capture card, which is connected to the streaming PC. The card captures, records, and encodes the output, which the streaming PC then uploads to Twitch. It's a bit of a luxury, obviously, but it's the best way to make sure that your stream never drops frames and is stable, giving your viewers the best experience possible.

PICK YOUR STREAMING CLIENT

Your livestreaming software—the program that encodes and uploads live video to your stream—is the heart of any broadcaster's content creation. Twitch's "Help" page (help.twitch.tv) maintains an updated list of all the livestreaming clients that are compatible with the site, but most people use either X-Split or OBS ("Open Broadcaster System").

TAKE ADVANTAGE OF HARDWARE-SPECIFIC SOFTWARE

If you're using purpose-built hardware, like a high-end USB microphone, there's a good chance that it will come with its own software that offers more customization than Windows does on its own. Using these programs isn't strictly necessary to get a decent-quality stream—your peripherals (microphones, cameras, etc.) will work just fine without them, and that's good enough for the vast majority of streamers—but these programs can give you more control over your content. The more time you spend streaming, and reviewing and improving your content, the more you'll understand the kinds of tweaks that hardware-specific software offers over out-of-the-box functionality.

HOT 🔥 FIX!

When you first start your Twitch channel, your viewers won't have access to quality settings—those are only given to Twitch partners and randomly selected affiliates. Streaming at a high resolution (like 1080P) can prevent viewers with mediocre internet from being able to view your stream. So, to make your stream as accessible as possible, it's smart to broadcast at 720P until Twitch awards your channel quality settings.

It's always worth taking a second to make sure you're using software that helps you acheive your goals.

	OBS	X-SPLIT
PROS	+ Open source software means lots of cool third-party applications + Absolutely, completely free	+ Superior audio-video quality + More options for local recording—saving a video file of your broadcast—which makes uploading to YouTube easier + More control over video and audio settings
CONS	- Less control over your audio-video settings - Somewhat less intuitive interface	- No third-party apps - You have to pay for some of the advanced features - Not open source

USE EXTENSIONS TO GIVE YOUR VIEWERS MORE VALUE

One of the coolest things about Twitch is how it allows you and your audience to interact with each other in lots of different ways. Twitch extensions are a big part of that. An *extension* is an interactive overlay that enhances your content to enrich the viewing experience. That can include things like real-time game data, channel notifications, minimaps, live games, and heat maps. Since Twitch doesn't develop these on its own, but, instead, relies on third parties to build them, there's a huge community of programmers and creators developing extensions for all kinds of purposes. These developers are constantly making new extensions, so it's worth keeping an eye on what other streamers are using to see if there's something that would fit with your own stream.

It's worth keeping an eye on what other streamers are using to see if there's something that would fit with your own stream.

WHAT DO I DO WHEN I'M ON-AIR?

While it might feel like something you're only doing for fun, the truth is that streaming is a skill. And, like any skill, you have to practice. You'll naturally get better over time, but many of the techniques I talked about in Chapter 2 apply to Twitch, too. Review your broadcasts. Make some notes. Get feedback from friends and other viewers. Take it seriously. Watching people better than you can help you figure out what they do well. Think about what they could do better. Here are some ideas to get you started.

> Smile a little bigger, be a little louder, wave your arms a little wider.

CULTIVATE A PERSONALITY PEOPLE WANT TO WATCH

Everyone is going to tell you to be yourself. And that's true; when you're faking it or trying too hard to project something you're not—or you just don't have your heart in it—viewers can tell! But being yourself onstream isn't quite the same as being yourself off-line. Just like actors will tell you that they have to exaggerate gestures and facial expressions, Twitch streamers need to play up these things, too. Twitch is about being yourself *even more* than usual—smile a little bigger, be a little louder, wave your arms a little wider. That all might feel a little awkward at first, but you'll get used to it and it'll come across as "normal" to your audience. If you doubt me, just watch my stream closely.

KEEP TALKING UNTIL IT'S A HABIT

Just like you have to be a little "more" yourself than usual when you're on-air, you're also going to have to get comfortable talking more than you would if you were playing without an audience. This is true even when no one is watching your stream—you never know when someone's going to drop by, and if you're totally silent, you're not giving them a reason to stick around.

◄ **PREVIOUS PAGES:** Playing *Call of Duty: Black Ops 4* during TwitchCon's Doritos Bowl in 2018.

As for what you should talk about, that's up to you. Talking about the game and the decisions you make is always a good strategy, especially if you're very good at the game you're streaming. That said, it's harder to pull off live commentary in some games than others—in a fast-paced game without many breaks like *Call of Duty*, chances are you're going to be too focused on the game to say anything coherent about your decision making. But if you're playing, say, *Hearthstone*, there's plenty of time for you to talk about your gaming strategies out loud (this might even help you play better!). Beyond in-game topics, you can always talk about music, movies, other games you love. Just stick to topics you know so you always come across as confident as possible. Remember: what you choose to talk about defines your brand, so make sure it's something you want to be associated with.

INTERACT WITH OTHER STREAMERS

Socializing with other streamers isn't just a good reason to stream. Beyond building new friendships, it will also help you create your community. Seek out other streamers both off-line and online. Hop on to their streams sometimes (and be sure to invite them on to yours). Doing so will expose you to new audiences and new streamers to play with. It also makes it easier for you to ask them to host your stream (see "Hosting," page 127) when they're off-line and you're online (and vice versa—pay it forward!). What's more, playing in groups is often an easy way to increase the amount of social interaction going on in your stream—since you'll need to communicate with your teammates, you can be sure you'll keep talking on camera!

WHAT **VIEWERS** WANT

The biggest question in streaming is "Why do viewers tune in?" The best answer I have is that they want to get something in return for sharing their attention with you. Sometimes viewers are eager to learn more about a game, sometimes they just want entertainment, and sometimes they're looking for inspiration. Others just want to be social and hang out in chat. But whatever their motivation for tuning in is, they need to feel like they're getting value from your stream—otherwise, there's no reason for them to come back. Always pay close attention to what your viewers seem to want and try to deliver—the best streamers know that the relationship between a broadcaster and their audience is really a conversation.

HOT 🔥 FIX!

You ever think, *Yikes—I shouldn't have said that!?* It happens to me more often than I'd like. But the truth is that Twitch is a mentally demanding activity, and when you're live for hours every day, chances are you're going to say something you regret or you don't mean at some point. When it happens—and it will—the best thing to do is apologize right away, move on, and try to do better. There's no shame in admitting an error—you just need to make sure your apology is sincere and those errors don't become the norm.

SOCIALIZE WITH YOUR AUDIENCE

In one study, researchers found that a majority of viewers tuned in to Twitch not to be entertained or get better or decide what games to buy, but just for the feeling of being social. That means it's important to interact with your viewers. Ask them questions, and listen to what they say. If someone's having a bad day, offer some words of encouragement. Say hello to as many people as you can and greet them by name, *especially* if they're a subscriber or donate to your channel. And consider checking out Twitch extensions that give you new ways to connect with your audience—you can find all kinds of ways to make them feel like they're connected to you and your other viewers.

HOSTING

Hosting is a great way to participate in the broader community of streamers, letting you build your platform and your community even when you're off-line, while also helping out other streamers. "Host mode" gives all off-line broadcasters the ability to host another streamer's channel when it's live. So your viewers get exposed to a new streamer, but have their own chat, separate from whatever streamer you're hosting. You can even hop into chat from time to time to stir up discussion. You can also ask your friends to host you when you're live and they're not, which will help show your content to new audiences. Just be sure to offer to host in return, especially if your channel starts to grow.

NINJA'S WAY

"

FIND LIKE-MINDED STREAMERS
If you've decided that you want to stream with other people, the next step is deciding *who* you want to stream with. When you're a smaller streamer, it's not too much of a detriment to your brand to stream with whomever you want. You don't have thousands of people expecting you to play with a certain person day in and day out. So when you're on the grind, playing with people who have even five or ten more viewers than you can help. In the best-case scenario, you can become friends and continue to build off each other's streaming platform and communities.

Once you get to a thousand viewers, things start to change. You have to ask, "Who do I want to be associated with?" And whether or not those people should have the same vision as you, same style of streaming, and stuff like that. Tim, Lupo, and I are on the same page: we never swear, and we embrace this family-friendly kind of thing, which was a conscious decision. In a nutshell, just play with the people who share the same goals and ideals as you. "

▶ **OPPOSITE:** Streaming with my buddies DrLupo, TimtheTatman, and CouRageJD on New Year's Eve in Times Square.

BUILD YOUR COMMUNITY

The thing that separates well-known streamers from casual ones is the community they build. When you're a streamer, you're creating a platform where others can gather and interact around a common interest. But fostering any community takes work—you need to consistently gather people in one "place" so that they start to get to know one another. Remember that your fans are some of your best ambassadors, and if they're passionate about you, they'll share your content with their friends, exponentially increasing your reach.

Discord (a free voice and text app built with gamers in mind) is a great way to get your community together in one place. You can think of it as a big chat room for your friends or fans where they can hang out, whether you're live or off-line. Even for small streamers, it's worth putting a link to a personal Discord in your Twitch profile. Not only is Discord useful for making sure that important announcements (like "Hey, I'm Live!" or "New Subscriber Emotes!") are going to get seen by the people that matter most, but gathering all your fans also enriches their connection to one another and lets you interact directly with them. Discord gives you a way to keep your community connected even when you're not online. Just be sure that you stay connected to them, too: hop in every now and then to talk to folks to see what they're up to—you'll be glad you did, and they will, too.

BE THE STREAMER **YOU** WANT TO SEE

When you're a streamer and you've got a community, you're also, like it or not, a role model. That means taking responsibility not just for yourself, but also the community you've built, and the strongest communities aren't built just

on shared interests, but shared *beliefs*. You can't control every individual fan, obviously, but you can try to define what your fandom is about. Do your best to set the tone, so that the conversations going on in your chat or Discord don't turn into a toxic cesspool. When new people join, encourage older fans to show them the ropes. Just because someone is inexperienced doesn't mean their interest in your stream or a certain game isn't genuine! The internet can be a mean place, but you have an opportunity to make it kinder.

Tips for Growing Your Stream

- **SET REASONABLE GOALS FOR YOURSELF,** and make them as clear as possible. Don't just aim to get more subscribers. Be even more specific, like: "I will have one hundred subscribers by the end of this year."

- **FIND A CLEAR-CUT ANGLE FOR YOUR STREAM.** Are you helping viewers find new games? Or showing them in-game tips and tricks? Do you want to play a single game and develop a rich story and tight-knit community over time? All these can work, but you can't do all of them at once. Reflect on what you're best at and stick to it. You're unique, which means you can make your broadcast unique, too.

- **PLAY GAMES YOU CARE ABOUT.** But I've never really played a shooter I didn't like, so that's what I focus on. If you're not passionate about the game you're playing, your audience probably won't get excited about what you're streaming, either.

- **BUILD A WISH LIST!** When your audience wants to see you succeed, they want ways to support you. They can tune in, spread your stream on their own social media profiles, subscribe, and give donations, but, when you're starting out, sometimes fans are willing to help you get gear to improve your content. A lot of small streamers have an Amazon wish list on their profile that includes hardware upgrades, new games to play, or anything else that can improve a stream.

- **STREAM CONSISTENTLY.** If you log on only when you feel like it, your viewers are going to think you're not taking it seriously and will take their attention somewhere else. Try to mark off a specific time on specific days when streaming can be your first priority.

- **DON'T IGNORE YOUR AUDIENCE!** They're here not just to watch you play, but to interact with you and one another. Participate in conversations, spark discussions, and react to your chat. Doing so will do wonders for making them feel like they're part of something bigger than themselves (and you'll feel that way, too).

- **YOU CAN'T SKIMP ON SOCIAL MEDIA.** Post on Twitter, Facebook, Instagram, Snapchat, or wherever else when you go live. If your viewers save clips of your best plays (or worst ones), ask them to tweet them at you and then retweet them. And be sure to engage with your audience directly—even a simple "like" can make someone's day.

- **PERSEVERE!** Almost every professional streamer knows what it's like to doubt themselves. Streaming is a wonderful hobby, but it's not always an easy one, especially when you're starting out. I streamed for years to a small audience, and never knew if I was going to make it big. But I did it because I loved streaming, and even if I didn't have thousands of subscribers, I drew strength from the community of loyal viewers I did have.

THE UPS AND DOWNS OF
STREAMING

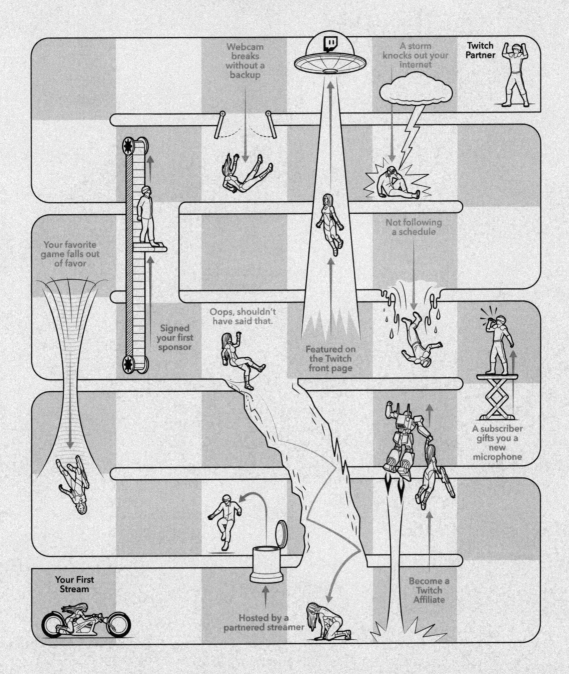

Webcam breaks without a backup

A storm knocks out your internet

Twitch Partner

Your favorite game falls out of favor

Signed your first sponsor

Oops, shouldn't have said that.

Featured on the Twitch front page

Not following a schedule

A subscriber gifts you a new microphone

Your First Stream

Hosted by a partnered streamer

Become a Twitch Affiliate

New Year's with Ninja

Planning for the Times Square event we did started when I was streaming at Lollapalooza the summer before, and I was approached by someone from (you guessed it) Red Bull. The guy said, "We have this killer idea. We want you to stream from Times Square on New Year's Eve." Honestly, my first thought was "How is that even possible? How can you make that safe and secure? Will people even like this?" But Red Bull's team said they'd found an amazing room and rented it out and that they wanted me to be there. So we decided to do it—it really wouldn't have been possible without their help.

When the time came, we flew to New York on December 29 to start preparing and to make sure that everything about the room was good. We wanted to make it as hype as we could, which meant making sure that I had a sick setup and space to interact with fans. The view was crazier than I could have imagined—right on the street in Times Square with huge windows all around. During the New Year's Eve show, we look outside and could see Ryan Seacrest. The streaming itself was similar to what it always is because I've done it at so many venues. But the atmosphere—all the people, the lights, the cameras, the rain, the music—that made it really memorable. And my whole family flew to New York to support me, as did some of my streaming friends—my other family.

But the most memorable part was probably walking in the rain with Jessica after we left the venue. We had security with us, but we got all the way to the main stage to be interviewed by somebody. Our outfits were totally soaked from the rain that night, but being able to walk past all these people and see their support—that was unforgettable. It just goes to show how much gaming matters to all kinds of people all over the world.

Let's face it: gaming can get a bad reputation. Chances are you've heard something about how gaming makes you antisocial, or leads to aggressiveness, or ruins your schoolwork. And, sure—there are a lot of problems in the world, and it's easy to blame games if you've never tried one. But that's not the gaming I know, and I'll bet it's not the one you do, either. At its best, gaming helps you meet friends, not lose them; it helps you relieve stress, not increase it; and it can make you a better, more effective person. **The truth is that gaming can help you live a better life,** and this chapter is about just that.

THE MENTAL GAME

It's tempting to think that everything that makes a gamer great has to do with their in-game skills, but what happens out of the game matters just as much as what happens inside it. Too often, I've seen the careers of extremely talented players ruined because they couldn't get a handle on their mental state or couldn't control their temper. Here's the truth: mental skills are gaming skills; social skills are gaming skills. What that means is that you can't separate gaming from the rest of your life—you have to see how they're intertwined for the better.

CULTIVATE A WINNING MIND-SET

Psychologists have spent a lot of time over the last decade to prove what gamers have known all along: that gaming is a mentally demanding activity. Playing well is as much about keeping your head in a good space as it is about developing your in-game abilities. That means that, if you want to play your best in-game, you need to take care of yourself outside of it. If you're not focused, if you're not motivated, if you don't have goals (short- or long-term), or you're lacking self-confidence, that's going to hurt your ability to play your best.

PUT IN THE RIGHT KIND OF EFFORT

It's important to match your mind-set to your actions. Practicing, competing, and playing casually are different activities, and each has its own headspace for you to get into. No one can do one of them all the time, but a lot of young players try to go into all three with the same kind of attitude. This leads to problems because your attitude and your actions are mismatched. If you're practicing with a casual mind-set, you won't see results. And if you're playing casually with a competitive mind-set, you're going to get frustrated, especially if you're playing with friends who just want to have fun. So before you start any kind of gaming session, take a moment to remind yourself what you're trying to achieve with it. I promise it will feel more purposeful, and you'll save yourself some frustration.

HOT 🔥 FIX!

Here's the thing about having a competitive mind-set: you have it or you don't. You don't have to have one to enjoy playing games, but if you're serious about being the best, your will to win is going to be the fire that keeps you fighting. In everything I've ever done—soccer, video games, whatever—I've always wanted to be the best. I hated when teammates would say, "Tyler, why are you so mad? It's just a game!" in the middle of an actual game. I'd reply, "What are you even doing playing if you don't actually care about the game?" Would you ever say, "It's just a game" to Tom Brady when he's playing in the Super Bowl? Of course not.

I'd be easier on myself if I didn't have that mentality, but I do. And I probably wouldn't be where I am today without it. These days, I'm better at understanding that not everyone shares that attitude, and that's okay. But you should really ask yourself: Why do you really want to be the best? What keeps you going? How are you always going to challenge yourself to improve? You can practice as much as you want, but unless you're hungry, you're not really going to see the results you want, and your time would be better spent just playing games, rather than trying to master them.

EVERYONE NEEDS DOWNTIME

If you're focusing on one game with all your energy, it's good to have a couple video games you can enjoy on the side. Maybe you've got a low-stress game that you like to go back to, or an MMO where you can drop in every once in a while, do some quests with friends. New games are always coming out, and it's worth trying new ones as they come out to stay on top of what's popular or even discover a new passion.

BALANCE YOUR LIFE

If you spend a lot of time watching my stream, you know how important my family is to me. My wife, Jessica, and my brothers are a huge part of my life and they remind me that there's a life beyond gaming. When I was starting out, I would get upset whenever someone walked in the room when I was streaming. But now, if one of my brothers wants to hang out, I'm happy to turn off the stream and spend time with them. Just like elite competitors have good all-around in-game skills, part of growing up is finding balance in your life. Sometimes people see playing games as opposed to "real life" while others see it as their *entire* life. Both are wrong, I think. Gaming is as much a part of your life as anything else is, so you don't have to choose. What you do have to do is make sure that it's helping, not harming, everything else you have going on—your family, your schoolwork, your social life.

NINJA'S WAY

" **WHEN I'M NOT PLAYING** *FORTNITE* **OR** *APEX LEGENDS* . . . *Final Fantasy XI* is hands down my favorite game. I've played it for my whole life, pretty much, and I think it made me into the person I am today. It was just a good MMO. It challenged you, and you couldn't do anything alone. You were forced to think critically, come up with strategies, and form certain parties to accomplish different tasks, so you had to have patience. I'd wait an hour or two just to be able to do one thing in-game. That was hard when I was twelve or thirteen, but it taught me a lot—about patience, about teamwork, about creativity, and so many other things. And it made me hella good at typing. "

This is true even when you're trying to go pro, but there are some other considerations. During the beginning of your career, you're going to have to make sacrifices—there were so many times when I wanted to spend time with my brothers or my wife, but I had to stay on my grind. Just make sure you don't sacrifice everything. Because the truth is that no professional gamer can do it on their own. I have a dream job, sure, but it's the people around me who help make it possible. I might be the only one onstream, but I couldn't do what I do without the support of my wife, my family, and my talent agency. What I'm saying is this: finding balance between gaming and the things that *aren't* gaming will actually help you become a better gamer, whether you want to stream or compete.

NINJA'S WAY

DEALING WITH STRESS I've got dog therapy. It's so funny because I'll have a really bad day and then I'll walk upstairs and they come up and start licking my face and I'm just, like, "You guys get me." It's like, "How could I be a bad person if these two dogs are just loving me?"

SET AND MEET GOALS

Achieving goals is one of the best ways to keep your motivation up. They're a tangible reminder that you really are improving and that the work you're putting in is worth it. Goals can be big or small, short- or long-term. But when you're challenging yourself, goals give structure to your life and your actions. Over time, that lets you turn little achievements into big ones.

BUILD SELF-CONFIDENCE

A few years ago, I read an interview with Jaedong—one of the best *StarCraft* players in history, and, for a while, the highest-earning gamer of all time. He was going through a slump and the interviewer asked Jaedong who he thought would win a tournament he was competing in. Jaedong replied that he goes into every tournament thinking that he's the favorite to win, because that's the kind of self-confidence you need to win. (He ended up winning that tournament, by the way.) I think he was right. What he's describing isn't always rational—sometimes you really aren't the favorite to win—but if you go into a match doubting your ability to come out on top, that's going to eat at you the whole time and hurt your ability to play effectively. *Believe in yourself* isn't just a slogan—it's a way of becoming the person you imagine yourself to be.

HOT 🔥 FIX!

AVOIDING TILT Anyone who has played video games knows what it's like to tilt—that irrational anger at yourself, or others, from some upsetting in-game event, which leads you to get frustrated and make even more unforced errors. It's a vicious cycle, and once you're in it, it's hard to get out.

The best thing you can do to avoid tilt is prevent it from happening in the first place. If you're already in a bad mood, stay away from whatever game you're taking seriously. Play something simpler, or a game that you're not as invested in, or do something else entirely. Alternatively, set a "hard" number of losses before you take a break—so, for example, if you lose three games in a row, take a fifteen-minute break and do something else.

Once you are tilting, though, the only real solution is to walk away. The problem with tilt is that it's a cycle: it makes you play worse, which will make you even more frustrated and likely to play *even worse*.

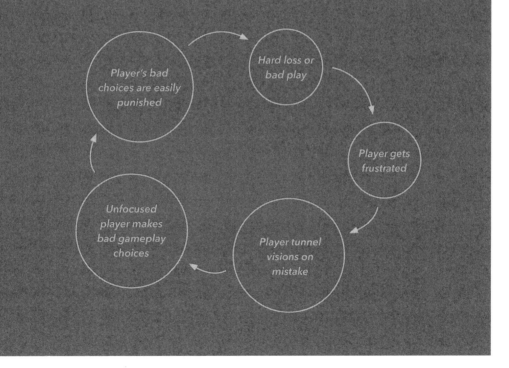

Player's bad choices are easily punished

Hard loss or bad play

Player gets frustrated

Player tunnel visions on mistake

Unfocused player makes bad gameplay choices

SMART Goal Setting

"SMART" goal making is a popular idea in a lot of life coaching that helps people develop, set, and reach their goals, whether they are short-term or long-term. Following is what each letter in the SMART acronym stands for and examples of how to change less helpful goals to better-defined goals.

Specific

It's no good setting vague goals because you won't actually be able to know when you've reached them.

BAD: Win more *Fortnite* games.

GOOD: Win at least one/two/etc. game(s) each day.

Measurable

Attaching a number to your goals is a great way to hold yourself accountable, and it also focuses your goals. Not everything can be broken down into a number, but these are useful for you to recognize what your goal really is and know when you've met it.

BAD: Be better at *Fortnite*.

GOOD: Improve my KDA (kills/deaths/assists ratio) by .5 over the next six weeks.

Attainable

There are dreams, and then there are goals. And while it's important to have both, you should be honest with yourself about what you think you can realistically achieve. If your goal is too much to handle, it will feel impossible and you'll just demoralize yourself. Challenge yourself, but within reason. Remember: you can always set bigger goals once you meet the smaller ones.

BAD: Beat Ninja at a LAN (local area network) event.

GOOD: Win a local tournament hosted at my school or a LAN cafe.

Relevant

Making sure your goals are relevant to you means taking a step back and asking *why* you want to achieve them. If you're taking your goals seriously, chances are that you're working toward something bigger—maybe it's winning a local tournament, or just improving a specific skill.

BAD: I'm trying to improve my building skills, so I'm practicing my tracking aim.

GOOD: I'm trying to improve my building skills, so I'm forcing fights in open areas.

Time-Related

When you're setting goals, try to think of them as either short-, medium-, or long-term goals. Be honest with yourself about what you think you can achieve in a few days, a few weeks, or a year or more. Goals build on one another: big goals require achieving a lot of little ones, but if you only focus on the little ones, you'll miss the big picture.

BAD: Get 100 new followers to my stream by next week.

GOOD: Grow my stream to 250 subscribers over the next twelve months.

NINJA'S WAY

DEALING WITH FRUSTRATION
Playing *League of Legends* is the first time I got introduced to the concept of tilting. It was about six years ago, and one of my buddies just told me, "Dude, you're tilted!" I was, like, "What are you talking about?" and he said, "You're playing stupidly, go take a break." And I realized I *was* playing stupidly. I was making dumb plays to try to make a point, even though I knew they weren't the right calls.

So I just hopped off for a bit—thirty minutes to an hour, probably. I got some food, watched a little television, took a walk and got some fresh air. There are lots of things you can do when you're tilted—take a shower, change your clothes, literally anything that will just reset your mind. If you can just get the game out of your head for a few minutes, then you're going to be in a good spot to say, "All right, let's get back to the grind."

MANAGE YOUR STRESS AND EMOTIONS

Let's face it. Gaming can be frustrating. If you're a really serious competitor like me, chances are that losing feels worse than winning feels good. And since you're going to lose sometimes, you need to find a way to deal with the negative feelings that come with it. Over the last couple of years, I've started to understand that it's okay and normal to get angry—but it's also important to understand that you're upset and take the right steps to get back in a good headspace. Too many gamers just get angrier and angrier and blame everyone but themselves.

CRITICISM: SHRUG IT OFF OR RESPOND?

Every day that I go online (which, you know, is literally every day), I know I'm going to read at least one mean comment about me. Probably hundreds across Twitch, Facebook, Twitter, and anywhere else on the internet. Even people who have subscribed to my channel will sometimes say really rude things like "you suck" or "you're bad at the game." And even though there's a part of me that wants to completely ignore these or never see them, that's just not going to happen, because no streamer ever got popular from ignoring their audience.

HOT 🔥 FIX!

It's easy to brush off criticism when you know it's untrue. When someone says I suck at *Fortnite*, I know that they're probably just jealous because I know I *don't* suck at *Fortnite* and I've got a couple thousand wins to prove it. But people do say things that get to me sometimes, usually because I know they're right. No one likes being wrong, but the truth is that we're all wrong sometimes. And that's okay. The question is how you respond. Remember that taking criticism to heart makes you look more, not less, competent. If you refuse to listen to your teammate or practice partner when they say, "Hey, that wasn't the right choice," then you're never going to improve. So you owe it to yourself—and everyone around you—to consider the possibility that you're wrong.

You don't have to choose between gaming and making the world a better place.

GAMING FOR GOOD

One of the best ways to show the world that gaming can be a force for good is to use gaming to support important social causes. Some of the most important things I've ever done have been the various charity events I've participated in over the course of my career like my stream supporting the American Foundation for Suicide Prevention. It feels great to know you're gaming for a good cause, of course, but these kinds of events also do wonders for helping out gaming's reputation in the public eye.

But you don't have to wait until you're well known to take part in a charity event. Instead, you should think about what you can do with the skills, passions, and resources you have now. If you love streaming, you can do a twenty-four-hour stream and collect donations for a good cause. If you're into esports, you can organize a charity tournament at a local venue. And if you're an excellent player, you can volunteer your time and skill to teach newer players in your community. You don't have to choose between gaming and making the world a better place.

EVERYONE'S A GAMER

· · · · ·

Not everyone plays the same games, of course, and not everyone plays the same way. But if you're looking for an art form that just about everyone has been involved in one way or another, games really do rank up there with film and music. If you're ever at a loss with how to connect with someone, there's a good chance you can get them to light up by talking about video games. Ask what they're playing and, no matter what they say, try to learn what they like about a game, even if it's one you don't have any interest in playing (chances are, they'll ask you next).

I really believe that there's no right way to be a gamer, and while it's tempting to think that competitive gamers like me are the only "real" gamers out there, competition is only one way out of many to engage with games. So make gaming a tool to connect with other people rather than splitting the world into gamers and nongamers. Because if there's one thing that's true about everyone on earth, it's that we all love to play.

NINJA'S WAY

WHAT I'D TELL MY THIRTEEN-YEAR-OLD SELF I'd go back and tell me to do exactly what I did. I still had time to play video games during middle and high school, for four hours a day, while getting As, Bs, and a couple of Cs, as well as being a full-time soccer player. Year-round, I had soccer practice and soccer games. But if I wasn't doing that, or doing homework, I was using that time to play video games. I had friends who were gaming with me, and that was a lot of my social life.

But I'd warn myself that when it became time for me to get really serious about games, I'd have to make some really tough decisions. There ended up being a lot of choosing between hanging out with friends, or going to a movie or a football game, and just staying home instead to put in the practice hours. At some point, I had to start making sacrifices and I wish I'd known I'd have to do that sooner.

Suite Times at the Super Bowl

The NFL actually reached out about having me do something with Super Bowl LIII a few months before the event. It was the NFL's one-hundredth season, so they wanted to do something special. Initially there were talks about me streaming during halftime, but we didn't think that we could make that cool enough for the fans, so we decided to just have me appear as a waiter in a commercial instead (it's on YouTube, if you haven't seen it!). I flew out to Los Angeles to film a couple takes with some big-name players and the NFL's commissioner, and they also offered Jessica and me some suite tickets. That's pretty much impossible to turn town, so we flew to Atlanta for the big game.

Our suite was actually right next to Steve Harvey's suite, and we had a ton of celebrity sightings. We rode the elevator up with Conor McGregor, and then Tyga was in our suite along with a couple big name Instagrammers and YouTubers. We were obviously excited just to be there and to see the Super Bowl in person, but, honestly, the coolest part of the entire night was the food. Oh my God, the food! We went tailgating at Guy Fieri's pregame beforehand—they had ten different stations, each with different things. One for barbecue, one for Chinese, a taco bar, one for burgers, and one with the best chicken wings I've ever eaten, period. There was also an auction for a hurricane relief charity; Jessica and I bought a few things, like a Tom Brady Jersey and helmets from the Lions.

With JuJu Smith-Schuster of the Pittsburgh Steelers, after shooting our cameo in the NFL100 commercial for the Super Bowl.

ACKNOWLEDGMENTS

You don't get to the top without surrounding yourself with the best. I want to take a moment to express my gratitude:

Thanks to the awesome team at Loaded, including Kyle, Colin, Justin, and Brandon, for guiding me along the way and helping me build my brand. You guys never fail to impress me with your creativity.

I'm grateful to my publishers at Penguin Random House—both at Clarkson Potter in the US and Ebury in the UK—for their expertise in publishing my first book. Special thanks to my skilled editors Angelin Borsics and Emma Smith; Mia Johnson, Nick Caruso, and Steve Leard for their vision; Chris Philpot for his awesome illustrations; Heather Williamson for proofing all the art; and Patty Shaw and Alison Hagge for crossing all my t's and dotting all my i's. And to Daniel Wikey, Lauren Kretzschmar, Stephanie Naulls, and Tessa Henderson for getting the word out about *Get Good* in a big way.

No one worked harder on this book than Will Partin, who is an excellent listener, deft writer, and a skilled gamer in his own right—and who worked on this book in the middle of writing his doctoral dissertation. Thanks for all your help in pulling the pieces together!

To the photographers whose fine work is featured in these pages, including Carlo Cruz, David Doran, Eric Espino, Benedict Evans, Joe Gall, Drew Gurian, William K, Ethan Miller, Robert Reiners, Leo Rosas, and Bartek Woliński. When you're streaming almost nonstop like I am, it's amazing to take a break and see my world through someone else's eyes.

Thanks especially to the team at Red Bull for being the best brand partner a guy could ask for. It's been a wild ride so far and I look forward to what's in store for the future.

I wouldn't be here if it weren't for my fans, who cheer me and build me up during every one of my streams. And to my gaming buddies, teammates, and competitors who always keep me on my feet. Thank you, my friends!

Thank you, Mom and Dad, for encouraging my interests in video games from the very beginning. To my brothers—my first competitors and teammates—I'll always look up to you. I love you all!

And to my biggest supporter, Jessica. Marrying you was my biggest win and I'll never take that for granted. I love you so much.

RESOURCES

LOGICAL INCREMENTS (LOGICALINCREMENTS.COM) is *the* place for looking up what's current in gaming hardware. Every month, they update their recommended list of what can be built with the latest hardware for every budget, from a few hundred dollars to a few thousand. If you're ready to build your own battlestation, this is the place to start.

1-HP (1-HP.ORG) is probably the most comprehensive guide to the physical elements of competitive gaming. They've got tons of articles and videos about everything from ergonomics to stretching exercises to nutrition, all carefully tuned to help gamers like you. Their goal is to help you play more and hurt less—need I say more?

POWER UP, TEAM UP, LEVEL UP

Lots of YouTube creators—not just the top competitive gamers—make great educational content about video games. If you like what you see, leave a comment saying so! It'll really make someone's day. You can also search for guides to your game directly in Google.

It's also important to try to keep your motivation high. One way to do that is read about your favorite streamers and their stories. The *Player's Tribune* and the *Player's Lobby* both help top streamers tell their stories from their perspective. If you're ever looking for direction, check those out to see how your heroes overcame the challenges they faced.

The popular stream coach—yes, that's a thing—Ashnichrist wrote *Build Your Dream Stream: The Ultimate Guide to Finding Your Voice, Growing Your Community, and Making Money as a Streamer.* It's a collection of wisdom that goes far beyond what I have space to discuss in this book. Also consider checking out her YouTube channel. It's got a massive archive of short videos on critical topics, like how to grow, how to make content your viewers want, and how to show your authenticity.

INDEX

Copyright © 2019 by Ninja Holdings, LLC

All rights reserved.
Published in the United States by Clarkson Potter/Publishers, an imprint
of Random House, a division of Penguin Random House LLC, New York.
clarksonpotter.com

"The NINJA" LOGO and related designs are used under license.

CLARKSON POTTER is a trademark and POTTER with colophon is a
registered trademark of Penguin Random House LLC.

Library of Congress Cataloging-in-Publication Data
is available upon request.

ISBN 978-1-9848-2675-6
Ebook ISBN 978-1-9848-2676-3

Printed in the United States

Interior design by Mia Johnson and Nick Caruso
Illustrations by Chris Philpot
Cover photo by Benedict Evans

Photography by:
Carlo Cruz / Red Bull Content Pool: pages 41, 71, 96, 105, 107, 110, 148
David Doran: pages 57, 91
Eric Espino, courtesy of NFL Enterprises LLC: page 151
Benedict Evans, courtesy of August Images: pages 2, 8, 10, 16, 24, 61,
    139, 144, 152, 156
Joe Gall / Red Bull Content Pool: pages 29, 33, 39, 47, 52, 85, 87, 88, 99,
    101, 102, 121, 132, 133, 134
Drew Gurian / Red Bull Content Pool: page 129
William K / Red Bull Content Pool: pages 76, 95
Ethan Miller, courtesy of Getty Images: pages 83, 137
Robert Reiners, courtesy of Getty Images: pages 4, 122
Leo Rosas / Red Bull Content Pool: pages 19, 80
Bartek Woliński / Red Bull Content Pool: pages 12, 59, 125, 154

10 9 8 7 6 5 4 3 2 1

First Edition